Nature's Masterpieces

The Earth, Its Wonders, Its Secrets

Nature's Masterpieces

THE READER'S DIGEST ASSOCIATION, INC.

Pleasantville, New York/Montreal

NATURE'S MASTERPIECES
Produced by Toucan Books Limited, London for
The Reader's Digest Association Limited, London
with Bradbury and Williams
Designer Colin Woodman

Written by Steve Cox
Consultant Editor Michael Bright
First English Copyright © 1994
The Reader's Digest Association, Limited

READER'S DIGEST PROJECT STAFF, US
Editor Kathryn Bonomi
Art Editor Eleanor Kostyk
Production Supervisor Mike Gallo
Research Assistants Mary Jo McLean,
Valerie Sylvester

READER'S DIGEST ILLUSTRATED REFERENCE BOOKS
Editor-in-Chief Christopher Cavanaugh
Art Director Joan Mazzeo
Operations Manager William J. Cassidy

Library of Congress Cataloging in Publication Data
Nature's masterpieces.
        p. cm – (The earth, its wonders, its secrets)
    Includes index.
    ISBN 0-89577-914-5
    1. Natural history. 2. Nature. I. Reader's Digest Association. II. Series.
    QH45.2.B7 1997
    508–dc21   97-22868

Address any comments about Nature's Masterpieces to
Reader's Digest, Editor-in-Chief, U.S. Illustrated Reference Books,
Reader's Digest Road, Pleasantville, NY 10570

To order additional copies of Nature's Masterpieces,
call 1-800-846-2100

You can also visit us on the World Wide Web at:
www.readersdigest.com

Printed in the United States of America

Second printing, September, 2000

FRONT COVER *Feeding lesser flamingos create stunning patterns of pink on blue on Lake Nakuru in Kenya. Inset: A crescent moon shines over Australia's dome shaped Olgas.*

PAGE 3 *Lesser flamingos in flight cast their shadows on the waters of Kenya's Lake Magadi.*

Contents

THE MIRACLE OF NATURE

Earth itself is a masterpiece, a well-tuned organism whirling through space. From hidden underwater worlds burgeoning with exotic life forms to the awesome destructive power of an erupting volcano, nature is never less than impressive.

Scientists who were cruising an area of the Pacific about 200 miles (320 km) off the Galápagos Islands in 1977 came across an astonishing oasis under the sea. They were searching for hot springs, often found near cracks in the seabed; what they discovered was an Alice in Wonderland community of creatures – none of which had ever been seen before – living in complete darkness some 8500 ft (2600 m) beneath the surface of the ocean. The animals included pink fish, the occasional purple octopus and shrimps with comb-like fronds where their eyes ought to be.

The first sign of their find came when remote-controlled cameras mounted on underwater sleds photographed areas of misty blue warm water inhabited by giant shellfish. A deep-sea submersible and its crew went down to investigate. The water was so deep that they took an hour and a half to drift slowly and very nearly blindly to the sea floor. At first they passed over barren lava rock, but as they approached a hot-water site they saw that it was shimmering like air over a

ICY DRAMA *Glacier power created the craggy landscape of South Georgia in the Antarctic.*

DESERT MASTERPIECE *Death Valley in California is the lowest place in the western hemisphere.*

warm pavement. Gushing from cracks in the ocean floor were fountains of hot water that turned a dirty blue as minerals precipitated out and stained the surrounding rocks. All around were thousands of deep-sea creatures. Giant clams and mussels up to 1 ft (30 cm) across were packed in dense clumps close to the vents. Close by were clusters of bright red tube worms, each about 3 ft (1 m) long. There were pure white crabs and squat lobsters.

The aquanauts had chanced upon a community perched on a platform of rock next to an underwater geyser. But what could the creatures be living on? The answer was soon found, since samples of water taken to the surface smelled of rotten eggs. Hydrogen sulphide forms in the hot water gushing from the vent, and marine bacteria feast on the sulphur. These in turn are food for other creatures in the vent food chain. Unlike other animal populations on Earth, the hydrothermal vent community is dependent not on the energy provided by the Sun, but on energy coming directly from the centre of the Earth.

More vent communities have since been found in other parts of the world, leading to speculation that hydrothermal vents, pouring from weak points in the Earth's crust, might possibly have been the sites where life was created more than 4000 million years ago.

THE DYNAMIC EARTH

Nature's masterpieces are varied and often surprising. They start with the Earth itself, a gigantic organism orbiting in space. The rocks beneath our feet are constantly moving, and have been for the past 4500 million years, since the formation of the Earth. Mountains and valleys, oceans and lakes, continents and islands have been formed, destroyed and re-formed, creating smaller, fleeting masterpieces of rock and water.

The nearest star, the Sun – a modest star as stars go – dominates our planet. Glowing red, orange and yellow in the sky, it is like a massive nuclear-fusion reactor that produces unbelievably large quantities of heat and light. It lies 93 million miles (150 million km) away, and yet its energy not only warms and stirs the oceans, but also provides sunlight which, through the remarkable process of photosynthesis in green plants, provides the energy to manufacture the basic food for most life.

At the same time, life as we know it depends totally on water. It was water that enabled life to make its first appearance between 4000 and 3500 million years ago in the primordial ocean. Our 'blue' planet is thought to be unique in the solar system in having water. Warmed by the Sun, the water in the oceans evaporates, rises high into the sky, and condenses in tiny droplets that collect on minute particles of dust to form clouds. The clouds are picked up by the winds and carried across the face of the planet, discharging their water as rain, hail and snow. Water and ice, sun and wind work like a giant sculptor, scouring the rocks, wearing them down and breaking off fragments to fashion the landscape.

The force of gravity then causes the water and ice to carry their rocky debris, in streams, rivers and glaciers, towards the sea. Here the debris settles on the seabed and is compressed into new rocks. These are pushed up to, and above, the level of the sea's surface by violent earth movements generated by vast quantities of heat energy from the natural furnaces at the centre of the Earth.

The ocean beds are rarely still, thanks to this activity at the centre of the Earth. The core of our planet has a temperature of about 4300°C (7770°F), generated by the disintegration of heavy radioactive elements such as uranium, thorium and potassium. The intense heat maintains the

NIGHT IN THE DEPTHS *Life may have started in 'vent' communities, such as this one off the Galápagos Islands.*

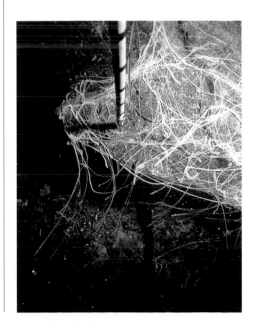

surrounding 'mantle' of molten rocks or magma almost at melting point. Floating on this is the skin of the crust.

The crust is divided into seven major plates, which are drifting about on the constantly moving, semi-liquid magma. Molten rock oozes up between the plates, cools, and adds to their size in a process known as 'seafloor spreading'. The overall effect is to push some continents apart. The Mid-Atlantic Ridge, dividing the eastern and western Atlantic, is one such spreading centre. It is pushing Africa and Europe away from North and South America at a rate of about 1 in (25 mm) every year. This is of great importance to

SYMPHONY IN PINK *Flamingos feed in Kenya's Lake Bogoria in the Great Rift Valley.*

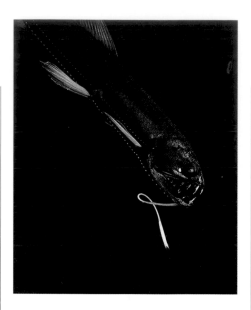

SPECIALISED IN RED *The stomiatoid fish, living in the ocean depths, is especially sensitive to red light.*

a particular population of submariners whose ancestors have been crossing the Atlantic for several million years.

TURTLE CROSSERS AND AN EXPANDING OCEAN

For most of the year, the green turtles of Brazil graze on underwater beds of eel-grass along the Atlantic coast, but when the time comes to mate and lay their eggs something extraordinary happens. Instead of swimming to highly desirable sandy beaches near their feeding grounds, some of the turtles head out into the South Atlantic and find Ascension Island, a tiny dot lying in the midst of a vast, featureless

ocean. How they find their way is a mystery and why they go at all is an even greater puzzle. Continental drift may offer a clue.

Millions of years ago, the ancestors of today's sea turtles probably laid their eggs on mainland beaches, at the mercy of the

newly evolving egg-eating mammals. As the seafloor spread, volcanic islands pushed up from it and their beaches of volcanic ash gave sea turtles a safer place to deposit their eggs. As the plate on which each island sat began to move away from the active centre, the sea wore it down until it disappeared below the waves. In the meantime, another volcanic peak rose behind it, and the turtles laid their eggs on this new island. To do so, however, they had to swim a little bit farther. Over the millenia, this process has been repeated again and again until the turtles of today have to swim over 1250 miles (2000 km) to breed. They find their way, it is thought, by following lines of force created by the Earth's magnetism.

Plate formation, however, cannot continue unchecked. If the plates continued to grow at spreading centres on the floors of the oceans, the entire planet would get bigger, but this is not the case. Instead, the plates overlap and are destroyed at so-called 'subduction zones' where one plate is pushed below another to be re-melted and re-absorbed into the mantle.

The actual size of the oceans, like that of the continents, is in a state of flux. The Atlantic is widening, while the Pacific is narrowing. The Mediterranean is in danger of becoming a lake, and the Red Sea is an embryonic ocean. In fact, the Red Sea is part of a gigantic tear across the Middle East and Africa known as the Great Rift Valley. It runs from Jordan and the Dead Sea in the north, through East Africa to Mozambique in the south. The rift was formed when the land between major faults sank. Since its formation, underground water has percolated up through a series of lakes strung out across East Africa.

Elsewhere in the Rift Valley, great lakes such as Lake Malawi and Lake Tanganyika are rich with fish, including the mouth-brooding cichlids – so named because they carry their eggs in their mouths until the eggs are ready to hatch. The land spreading out around is dominated by dramatic volcanoes such as Kilimanjaro and Kenya. The 100 sq mile (260 km²) extinct crater of Ngorongoro plays host, like an enormous natural safari park, to large numbers

of animals: elephants, hippos, hyenas, lions, cheetahs and wild dogs.

At nearby Olduvai Gorge, the river has sliced down through layer upon layer of volcanic ashes and sedimentary rocks and exposed fossil-bearing strata. Among the fossils of early lions, hyenas and other creatures lie the scattered remains of humanity's earliest known ancestors. The African rift was, perhaps, the biblical Eden – the cradle of humankind.

WHERE THE EARTH TEARS APART

Elsewhere, continental plates collide and buckle as one plate slams into another. The Himalayas, for example, rise where the Indo-Australian plate is pushing against the Eurasian plate. In places like these, sedimentary rocks – rocks formed at the bottom of the sea – are folded, twisted, warped and pushed

FOLDED SKYWARDS *'Folding' of the Earth's surface created the great peaks of the Himalayas.*

SNOW ON THE EQUATOR *Snow caps Kilimanjaro, Africa's highest peak, just 3° south of the Equator.*

high into the sky to form young mountain chains such as the Andes, Rockies and Alps as well as the Himalayas.

Violent, and sometimes devastating, reminders of the power that lies behind these gargantuan clashes are earthquakes and volcanoes. The biggest and most frequent quakes occur in zones close to plate boundaries, such as the San Andreas Fault in California. Here the Pacific and North

PADDING IN THE SNOW *The Himalayan snow leopard has adapted to life in the heights.*

American plates are sliding past each other. Los Angeles and the Baja Peninsula in Mexico are sitting, not on the North American plate, but on the eastern edge of the Pacific plate, and they are moving in a north-westerly direction. San Francisco, by contrast, sits on the western edge of the American mainland plate. The sliding process is not a smooth and continuous one: for most of the time the two plates are locked together by friction; but the forces driving them in different directions will not be denied. Tension builds up to the point where the friction is suddenly overcome. The plates lurch along their appointed paths, and the world hears of another earthquake.

The San Andreas Fault is just one section of an active circle of earthquake zones and volcanoes, known as the 'Ring of Fire', that surround the Pacific Ocean. In the north-west, Russia's Kamchatka Peninsula is dominated by volcanoes, and in the north-east lies Alaska's Valley of the Ten Thousand Smokes – a fiery landscape of hot springs, smoking vents and volcanoes. Farther south there are a string of the most dangerous volcanic peaks in North America, including Mount St Helens.

On May 18, 1980, the entire north side of Mount St Helens blew out. Some 6 ft (2 m) of ash and rock buried the immediate landscape, while volcanic debris and water from lakes, rivers and melted glaciers caused giant mud flows. It was estimated that 11 million fish, 27 000 grouse, 11 000

hares, 6000 black-tailed deer, 5200 elk, 1400 coyotes, 300 bobcats, 200 black bears and 15 mountain lions were killed. Despite early warnings 57 people lost their lives. Among the survivors were pocket gophers, burrowing animals that were safe in their tunnels. But nature abhors a vacuum and soon after the eruption muskrats, mink, deer, mice, frogs and newts and a variety of insects, centipedes and spiders quickly moved in to establish new homes.

Volcanically active areas are not always tainted with death and destruction. They can also be havens for living creatures. In Yellowstone National Park, for example, the winters are usually very harsh, and deep snow covers most of the land. Yet conditions are sufficiently balmy around its 200 geysers, 10 000 or more hot springs and bubbling mud pools, for bison, elk and moose to find carpets of sedges and grasses where they can feed and survive.

Many of the most violent volcanic eruptions known to humankind occur amongst the many islands sandwiched between the Pacific and Indian oceans. In

this geologically complex region, several plate boundaries meet. The most famous explosion was the one that ripped the volcanic island of Krakatoa apart in 1883. The explosions were heard 2200 miles (3540 km) away in Australia and giant tsunamis or tidal waves over 120 ft (37 m) high engulfed coastal villages in the Indonesian islands of Java and Sumatra, drowning 36 000 people. About 5 cu miles (21 km^3) of rock fragments were thrown into the air, and the surrounding region was temporarily plunged into darkness because of the fine ash in the atmosphere. The dust then travelled around the globe several times, giving rise to spectacularly red sunsets in many parts of the world throughout the following year.

ASH AND THE CLIMATE

The effects of volcanic ash on weather and climate have long interested scientists. In the 18th century, the American statesman and scientist Benjamin Franklin noted the connection between volcanic eruptions and changes in the weather. He was in Europe not long after southern Iceland split open along an 8 mile (13 km) stretch, spouting incandescent fountains of lava at

DANGER ZONE *The San Andreas Fault stands out clearly in the Carrizo Plains north of Los Angeles.*

ASH AND HOT GASES *Volcanic cloud shrouds Mount St. Helens during its 1980 eruption.*

a rate said to have rivalled that of water over the Niagara Falls. It was the largest outpouring of lava in modern times, and a thick, bluish haze of sulphur dioxide, dust and other volcanic gases settled over the island. Three-quarters of Iceland's livestock died, and 10 000 people – about a quarter of its population – perished during what came to be known as the 'Haze Famine'. The cloud reached south into Europe, partly blotting out the Sun and causing the severe winter of 1783–84. Franklin noticed the haze and made the connection between it and the bad weather.

Many years later, in 1815, his ideas were vindicated when the Indonesian volcano Mount Tambora blew its top, throwing vast quantities of ash into the atmosphere. More than 10 000 people on Sumbawa island were killed in the explosion and 38 000 died of hunger and disease the following year. The results of the eruption were noticed all over the world. Some of the English painter J.M.W. Turner's masterpieces, in which the 19th-century landscapist demonstrated an original use of light and colour, were thought

ALL STEAMED UP *A geyser shoots clouds of steam into the air in Yellowstone Park.*

to have reflected the after-effects of the eruption. From June until October in 1815, England experienced brilliant sunsets and colourful skies at twilight.

An even more massive eruption at Toba in Sumatra about 73 500 years ago has been implicated in the start of the last Ice Age. The explosion threw vast quantities of fine debris an estimated 16 miles (25 km) into the atmosphere, and although the dust itself settled out in a few months, sulphurous aerosols (clusters of fine particles suspended in the air) remained. This reduced the level of sunlight reaching the surface of the planet for several years. In higher latitudes, it resulted in temperatures 10-15°C (18-27°F) cooler than had been usual, and there was year-long snow cover over northern lands. Ice sheets covered much of North America, northern Asia and Europe as far south as the site of London. The sea level dropped considerably and a land bridge formed between North America and Asia, across which the first people travelled from Asia.

STORM CLOUDS AND TORNADOES

The interaction between sea and sky is the engine that drives the world's climate. This is another of nature's masterpieces,

CLIFFS OF ICE *A glacier from Alaska's Fairweather Range meets the sea in 100 ft (30 m) ice walls.*

though sometimes a destructive one, since it creates weather systems that can be just as devastating in their impact as volcanoes and earthquakes. Tropical cyclones, known as hurricanes or typhoons, are powered by the heat energy stored up in air passing over warm tropical seas. Strong winds blow around them in a tight spiral at speeds of up to 160 mph (257 km/h). They demolish virtually everything in their path and push up coastal sea surges that drown low-lying land.

In regions such as the Midwestern states of the USA hot, moist air rising in an upward spiral can quickly build into a narrow funnel with wind speeds reaching some 300 mph (483 km/h) to form one of the most frightening of weather phenomena: the tornado. It sweeps across the land, moving along at speeds of up to 37 mph (60 km/h) like a gigantic vacuum cleaner, sucking up everything in its path.

When storm clouds build up rapidly to heights of 6 miles (10 km) or more, a great mass of water and ice is carried within the clouds, supported by strong updraughts of air. These characteristic anvil-shaped cumulonimbus clouds warn of a thunderstorm. Within storm clouds the freezing and melting of water droplets leads to an enormous build-up of electrical charges that can be released from cloud to cloud as bright sheet lightning or from cloud to ground as spectacular and sometimes dangerous forked lightning.

In hot, parched desert lands rain brings about a sudden miracle. Flash floods and mud streams liberate an aromatic perfume

FISH IN MOUTH *The river-dwelling gharial of northern India can grow up to 15 ft (5 m) long.*

as the water revives dry and withered desert plants. Flowers blossom in an outburst of vivid colours. Frogs, which may have been cocooned for several years below the barren surface, fill the once silent air with belches and croaks. Shrimps, mosquitoes and water fleas magically appear in short-lived pools. Animals court, mate and reproduce in a frantic rush to complete their life cycles before the desert takes over once more.

In the colder parts of the world, the

IN THE FAST STREAM *Torrent ducks live in the whitewaters of South America's southernmost rivers.*

moisture in the clouds falls as snow that transforms rocky landscapes into smooth, brilliant white blancmange. In mountain areas, warm winds disturb the accumulations of snow perched precariously high on the slopes and trigger another of nature's killers – the avalanche. The destructive force can be so enormous that entire forests are swept away.

In parts of the world where snow falls faster than it melts, glaciers and ice sheets are formed. Snow falls upon compacted snow to build up thick layers of ice which in higher latitudes may bury huge areas. Three-quarters of the surface of Greenland is covered by a gigantic ice dome over 7000 ft (2134 m) thick at the centre.

In many parts of the world the ice sheets and glaciers of colder times have long gone but their legacy remains. The smooth, rounded rocks of the islands of the Stockholm Archipelago in the Baltic Sea were carved by ice. The largest lakes in the world – the Great Lakes of North America – were scooped out during pre-glacial times, but owe their present size and shape to the powerful grinding action of the retreating ice sheets.

AT HOME IN LAKES AND RIVERS

Isolated from other large bodies of water, many of the world's lakes have unique or unusual animals living on their shores or in their depths. Lake Baikal in Siberia is

the deepest freshwater lake in the world with a depth of 5314 ft (1620 m). It has its own species of freshwater seal, and its depths are home to freshwater sponges.

Lake Titicaca in South America is the world's highest large lake and lies in an immense basin 12 500 ft (3810 m) above sea level. It has a unique foot-long (30 cm) species of frog. Lake Nicaragua, the largest lake in Central America, was thought to have been cut off from the sea by a volcanic eruption and contains freshwater sharks, swordfish and tarpon.

Whether the ancestors of these fish, which are normally found in the sea, were trapped in the lake when it was formed and then gradually adapted to freshwater as the salinity of the lake changed, is not clear. Shark experts believe that the sharks, which are almost certainly bull sharks, are not permanent residents but instead visit the lake periodically. They probably use the 112 mile (180 km) San Juan River

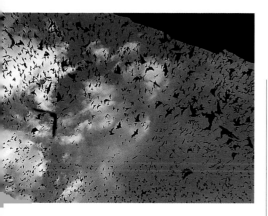

BATS IN THE CAVE *Bats gather at the mouth of Carlsbad Caverns in New Mexico.*

which drains from Lake Nicaragua to the Caribbean Sea.

The world's longest rivers also have distinct species of animals – some leftovers from the days of the dinosaurs. The Indus and Ganges rivers have the toothy, long-snouted gharial, a member of the crocodile family. The Amazon and Orinoco are home to caiman (another kind of crocodile), anacondas, giant arapaima – 15 ft (4.5 m) freshwater fish – and ferocious piranhas. The Mississippi has catfish and alligators, and the Danube and the Volga are famous for their sturgeon.

Some of the large rivers of the tropics have their own primitive freshwater dolphins. The Amazon has the boutu, a dolphin that has been known to co-operate with local fishermen to herd and catch fish, and the La Plata estuary has the franciscana, one of the smallest of the dolphins, just 6 ft (2 m) long. The susu of the Ganges and the Indus River dolphins are blind. To find their way about in the muddy water and to locate food, they rely partly on touch, using their sensitive front flippers, and partly on a sophisticated echo-location 'sonar' system that they share with sea-going dolphins.

Food and safety are the main reasons most animals head for river mouths. Sediments washed down by rivers are deposited in banks and deltas, and estuary muds are rich in worms and other marine invertebrates that provide a feast for hosts of waders and sea birds. In the shallows, mangrove swamps are nursery sites for various fish and other marine life. Among other things, the mangroves' tangle of roots are a favourite refuge for enigmatic

DECEPTIVE LOOKS *The whale shark (above) seems fearsome but it eats only small fish and plankton. The slow lava flows of Mauna Loa (below) pose little danger to people living nearby.*

mudskippers – a remarkable kind of fish that can survive in both air and water.

A river estuary with a narrow mouth and a great tidal rise and fall produces a bore. At high tide, particularly during powerful spring tides, a flood surges into the estuary, creating a high, precipitous wave that sweeps upstream. Large bores occur regularly in the River Severn in Britain, the Petitcodiac River, which empties into the Bay of Fundy in New Brunswick, the Hooghly River in West Bengal, Cook Inlet's Turnagain Arm in Alaska, and the River Seine between Rouen and Le Havre in France.

In eastern China, the bore of the Fuch'un River, which flows into Hangchou Bay on the edge of the East China Sea, speeds along at 15 mph (24 km/h) with a tidal wave about 10 ft (3 m) high. Stories abound of Chinese river folk utilising the power of the advancing wave. Sheltering

their boats in inlets dug out of the riverbanks they used to wait until the bore passed by and then set sail, riding the bore upriver. In 1888 and 1892, the British naval officer Commander W. Usborne Moore observed the technique. He saw 30 junks swept along, their sails set but their bows pointing in every conceivable direction. Some were even going backwards.

BLIND FISH IN LIMESTONE CAVES

In karst or limestone areas, a waterfall can simply disappear through a hole in the ground, the gateway to a wildlife community that lives its entire life in total darkness. The caves can be enormous. Those at Mulu in Borneo and at Carlsbad in New Mexico are true masterpieces, the size of cathedrals. Cave visitors, such as bats and cave swiftlets, use the relatively safe ceilings for nesting and roosting. Each dawn and dusk, entrances are bustling with the swirl of animals – swiftlets taking the day shift, bats on the night shift. In the innermost caverns are the permanent inmates. No daylight means that eyes are

redundant, and so many cave residents are blind, relying on touch, smell or echolocation to find food. There are blind cavefish, beetles, centipedes, crayfish and salamanders, all locked away and isolated from the outside world.

In the West Indies, cave systems carved out thousands of years ago by freshwater rivers and streams were drowned by the sea. The great ice sheets melted at the end of the last Ice Age, about 10 000 years ago, and the sea level rose by over 200 ft (60 m). The result was the 'blue holes' of the Bahamas and of the barrier reef of Belize. Seen from the air they appear as large, circular, dark blue holes in the sea floor. They stand out clearly from the pale-coloured coral reef surrounding them. Each hole is about 350 ft (100 m) deep and has side passages branching from the main shaft. While the deeper caverns of the blue holes are dark and mainly devoid of life, the upper sections are encrusted with a great diversity of corals, sponges, seaweeds and sea fans.

The largest reef system in the world is

the 1250 mile (2000 km) Great Barrier Reef of Australia. Five days or so after the December full moon each year all the corals on the entire reef spawn at the same time. The sea is turned into soup as the coral polyps release packages of sperm and eggs. Synchronised spawning occurs on other reefs, too.

The coral polyps themselves fall prey to the crown-of-thorns starfish, which has undergone a population explosion and is destroying the Australian reefs. Why this spiny monster has increased so dramatically in numbers is still a mystery, but it is a reminder of the constant battle between the forces that create new land and the forces that destroy it.

In the centre of the Pacific Ocean just such a battle is fought daily. The Hawaiian islands are directly over a 'hot spot' in the Earth's crust. Below the thin ocean crust, a plume of superheated magma rises close to the surface and molten rock bursts out. As the Pacific plate passes over the plume, great free-flowing basaltic volcanoes erupt above the surface of the sea to form large islands. But the plate on which they sit moves steadily westward, like a giant conveyor belt, at a rate of about 3¹/₂ in (9 cm) per year. The volcanoes slide away from the hot spot and eventually become extinct. The sea then takes over, and wind

and waves pound the islands until they disappear below the surface.

The islands are also a natural laboratory where scientists are able to study the process of evolution. Thousands of years ago, animals and plants flying or drifting from the mainland colonised the islands and evolved independently of their relatives elsewhere. One of the many Hawaiian islands, for example, was the landfall for a species of finch-like bird that had crossed more than 1860 miles (3000 km) of ocean from South America. Finding little competition for food and living space, the birds bred and spread, but as they began to specialise in collecting locally abundant foods they evolved into

DESERT LIVING *The onymacris beetle (left) of the Namib Desert gathers all available moisture. Sand dunes spread out in California's Death Valley (above).*

separate species. Each developed a specialised bill to exploit a different food. Today, Hawaii has many species of these finches, known as honey creepers. Some remain as seed-eaters with stout finch-like bills, while others, with more pointed bills, specialise in catching insects and grubs. Some of the birds have taken to sipping nectar. There are berry-eaters, and those which break open sea birds' eggs.

Similarly, in the Galápagos Archipelago off the coast of Ecuador in the eastern Pacific, mainland finches have evolved into quite distinct species, including a bird that uses a cactus spine as a 'tool' to prise out insect larvae, and another that, like a vampire bat, drinks blood – in this case, of seabirds. It was on these isolated islands that the 19th-century British naturalist Charles Darwin was able to observe the work of evolution in action, and use it as evidence to support his theories.

ADAPTING TO DROUGHT

In hot deserts, animals have developed some inventive ways for collecting enough water to survive. In the Namib Desert of Namibia, for example, where fogs drift in from the South Atlantic, the tiny onymacris

ICY WILDERNESS *Wright's Valley in Antarctica is one of the driest places on Earth.*

MAGIC OF THE MOON *Pintail ducks are etched against a full moon.*

beetle is a miniature masterpiece of adaptation that stands on its head to allow the moisture collecting on its body to drip down to its mouth.

Some of the driest places on Earth are not in hot deserts but in the deep-freeze. They are the dry valleys of the Antarctic. These barren tracts of land have few visible signs of life. Lichens and algae live hidden and protected within the rocks of the valley slopes, but on the floor all that can be seen are the dried, shrivelled corpses of seals and penguins that have lost their way.

Surrounding this cold white, almost totally sterile wilderness are seas that overflow with life. The Southern Ocean is rich in nutrients and consequently in wildlife. Penguins and seals stay the whole year round. Some, like emperor penguins and Weddell seals, dive to great depths where they collect squid and fish. Giant baleen whales, such as the slow-swimming, white-winged humpbacks, are summer visitors. They feast mainly on krill – tiny shrimp-like crustaceans. They must feed well for when they return to the tropics to breed they do not eat for nine months.

Much of what takes place on the Earth is influenced by forces outside our planet. The Sun sets biological rhythms, so that animals and plants know what to do and when. It provides, too, a beacon by which

migrants can chart their paths across the world or by which foragers, such as bees and ants, can find their way home. In similar fashion, the stars in the night sky guide nocturnal wanderers. Life along the shore, meanwhile, is dominated by twice-daily tides created by the gravitational pull of the Moon.

Extraterrestrial forces may also provide the impetus for sudden spurts in evolution or bring life to an abrupt end. Some scientists now believe that mass extinctions are a regular occurrence, coinciding with the arrival of comets, asteroids and meteorites that, like Earth, have been orbiting the Sun but which are on a collision course with our planet. A direct hit not only makes a large dent in the Earth's surface, but the clouds of dust and ash obscure the Sun and make living impossible for many species of plants and animals. One such collision, though not with Earth, occurred in July 1994 when the comet known as Shoemaker-Levy smashed into the planet Jupiter. Every 26 million years, according to some calculations, a catastrophe of this kind forces a proportion of life on Earth into extinction, and the vacuum is filled by the

RECORD IN STONE *Mollusc fossils leave their trace in the rock in Somerset, England.*

rapid evolution of the survivors. In this way, so the theory goes, evolution progresses in a series of fits and starts.

The greatest of these mass extinctions was at the end of the Permian Age, about 250 million years ago, when up to 96 per cent of all life on Earth was wiped out. The most famous such event, however, was just 64 million years ago, at the end of the Cretaceous period, when the dinosaurs and their relatives became extinct.

Scientists know that these extinctions took place because the rocks tell them so. Embedded in the rocks are the remains of plants and animals that once lived on our planet. The presence or absence of these fossils not only indicates which species of plants and animals were living at any time, but also gives a clue to the weather. At the time the dinosaurs disappeared, fossilised plant material provides evidence that there was a dramatic shift in the world's vegetation. The rocks contain fossilised pollen that shows that pollen from flowering plants dropped significantly, while the number of fern spores increased. This change in vegetation 65 million years ago is reminiscent of the aftermath of a forest fire today. Whatever killed the dinosaurs, it seems, scorched the Earth.

The entire history of the Earth is locked up in rocks. The strata are like pages in a gigantic natural-history book. In each chapter, the fossil record tells us how life-forms, landscapes and climates have come and gone, an indication that even the most robust of nature's masterpieces are not permanent residents but fleeting guests in a volatile universe.

RESTLESS NATURE

1

NATURE AS ARCHITECT *Water created Delicate Arch in Utah's Arches National Park.*

LANDSCAPES ARE CONSTANTLY CHANGING, AS NATURE'S ENDLESS CYCLES CREATE AND DESTROY, COMPRESS AND STRETCH, MOULD AND ERODE. VOLCANOES AND GIGANTIC EARTH MOVEMENTS PUSH UP MOUNTAINS, RIDGES AND PLATEAUS, WHILE ICE, WATER AND WIND GRIND THEM DOWN AND RESHAPE THEM INTO VALLEYS, PLAINS, CAVES AND CANYONS. GLACIERS ETCH DEEP SCARS IN THE EARTH'S SURFACE AND RIVERS ERODE MEANDERING PATHWAYS TO THE SEA. SHAPED BY THE ELEMENTS OVER THOUSANDS OF YEARS ROCKS ARE HONED AND SMOOTHED, CREATING GIANT SCULPTURES THAT DOMINATE THE LANDSCAPE. NEW ISLANDS, FORMED BY THE ACTIVITIES OF TINY CORALS, PUSH UP GENTLY BUT STEADILY THROUGH THE WAVES.

ITALIAN GLORY *Sun sets over Italy's Dolomite Mountains.*

EVOLVING LANDSCAPES

Heat and molten rock rise from the Earth's depths to shape an ever-moving landscape. Earth's crust is never still, and its movements have created scenery as varied as coral atolls in the Pacific and surreal limestone towers in south China.

Every year, Europe and America drift a few inches farther apart. By contrast, the Pacific on the other side of the globe is shrinking slightly. In the Earth's rooftop, the mighty peaks of the Himalayas are creeping slowly higher as the decades go by.

The Earth's crust is constantly on the move. The theory of 'plate tectonics' – one of the most significant discoveries of 20th-century science – shows that the surface of the Earth is divided into seven large segments or plates. Over millions of years, the movements of these plates have shaped the patterns of the oceans and continents, and laid the foundations for all the world's landscapes. Where they collide – as where the Indian plate meets the Asian – one pushes underneath the other, and in the resulting upheaval mountains are formed. This is how the Himalayas came into being, and India is still forcing its way beneath Asia, pushing up the mountains with it, so that in 1990 Mount Everest was 10¹/₂ in (270 mm) higher above sea level than it was in 1900.

The Earth is, in fact, like a massive furnace – with temperatures of around 4300°C (7770°F) at its centre. This is partly because it was formed at a very high temperature some 4.6 billion years ago and is still cooling. The interior is insulated by thick layers of molten mantle rock and by the thin, solid outer layer of the crust, both of which act like the lagging around a hot-water tank.

The crust consists of the ancient continental crust on which we live, and the

BUILDING EARTH'S MOUNTAINS

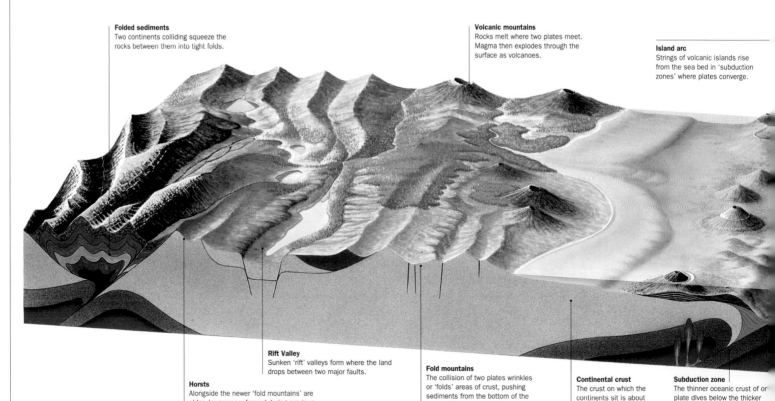

Folded sediments
Two continents colliding squeeze the rocks between them into tight folds.

Volcanic mountains
Rocks melt where two plates meet. Magma then explodes through the surface as volcanoes.

Island arc
Strings of volcanic islands rise from the sea bed in 'subduction zones' where plates converge.

Rift Valley
Sunken 'rift' valleys form where the land drops between two major faults.

Horsts
Alongside the newer 'fold mountains' are older, lower ones, formed during previous earth movements.

Fold mountains
The collision of two plates wrinkles or 'folds' areas of crust, pushing sediments from the bottom of the sea up above sea level.

Continental crust
The crust on which the continents sit is about 25 miles (40 km) thick.

Subduction zone
The thinner oceanic crust of one plate dives below the thicker continental crust of another.

younger, heavier and darker crust that covers the floor of the oceans. The continental crust is around 25 miles (40 km) thick, while the ocean floor is only around 3 miles (5 km) thick.

Running along the centre of the ocean floor are 'mid-ocean ridges', a massive underwater string of mountains that mark the sites of deep-sea volcanic activity. Molten rock rises from the mantle and bursts through into a dark underwater world, where it cools rapidly to form hard rock. As new lava erupts, the old hard rock is pushed aside; the new rock generated thus gradually spreads the ocean crust a few inches every year.

Heat moves from the interior of the Earth to the surface in a series of gigantic convection currents – that is, currents caused by the transfer of heat. These behave rather like a pot of porridge on the stove. A convection current in the middle makes the hot porridge in the centre of the pan rise, and the cooler porridge around the sides sink. After a while, the surface forms a skin – like the Earth's crust – that moves sluggishly towards the edges of the pan.

In much the same way, the Earth's convection currents rise through the mantle, melting rocks to form the mid-ocean ridges. They then move horizontally away from the ridges, dragging the newly formed crust – like the skin of the porridge – with them across the floor of the oceans.

THE HIGHEST *Mount Everest is still slowly rising above sea level.*

EARTH'S PLATES *Seven plates make up the Earth's crust.*

PUSHED FROM BELOW *Earth's great mountain ranges, from the Himalayas to the Rockies to the Alps, testify to the power at work in its interior. They form where continental plates meet, wrinkling the crust and pushing rocks that once lay on the sea bed thousands of feet into the sky.*

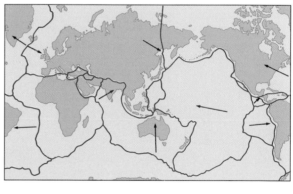

Ocean trench
A deep scar, known as an 'ocean trench', forms in the bottom of the ocean along the subduction zone.

Atoll
Rings of coral reefs form on the shoulders of a volcanic island.

Seamount
Underwater 'seamounts' are all that remains of a volcanic island whose volcano has become extinct and then been eroded by the sea.

Mid-ocean ridge
Magma oozes through cracks in the oceanic crust and creates 'mid-ocean ridges'.

Oceanic crust
The crust covered by the oceans is around 3 miles (5 km) thick.

Convection currents
Movements of the magma below the crust cause the plates of the Earth's crust to move.

KILAUEA IN ACTION   *Earth's heat engine carries on shaping Hawaii.*

Eventually, the heat is lost, and the cooling currents dive back down into the mantle – just as the porridge sinks around the edges of the pan.

The new crust moving along the sea floor makes oceans such as the Atlantic widen by about an inch (25mm) every year. But there is also a limit to this movement. Around the fringes of the Pacific Ocean, in the so-called Ring of Fire, the ocean crust follows the descending convection current and plunges back into the mantle. As it does so, it causes earthquakes, with fractures and faults forming in the brittle crust above; it is also a zone of volcanoes. As the ocean floor is slowly carried down into zones like this (known as 'subduction' zones), the continents on either side gradually move closer together.

FIERY ERUPTIONS IN THE PACIFIC OCEAN

VOLCANOES CREATED THE ISLAND

PARADISE OF HAWAII

Kilauea is one of three active volcanoes on the Pacific island of Hawaii – the largest island of the Hawaiian chain. Along with

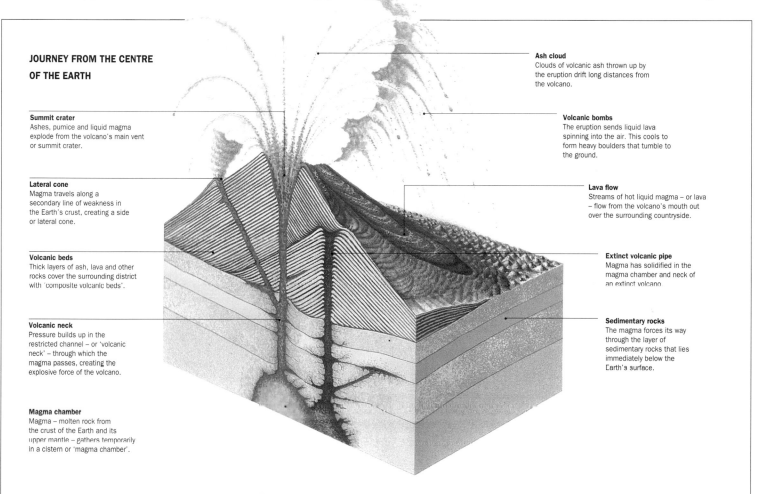

JOURNEY FROM THE CENTRE OF THE EARTH

Summit crater
Ashes, pumice and liquid magma explode from the volcano's main vent or summit crater.

Lateral cone
Magma travels along a secondary line of weakness in the Earth's crust, creating a side or lateral cone.

Volcanic beds
Thick layers of ash, lava and other rocks cover the surrounding district with 'composite volcanic beds'.

Volcanic neck
Pressure builds up in the restricted channel – or 'volcanic neck' – through which the magma passes, creating the explosive force of the volcano.

Magma chamber
Magma – molten rock from the crust of the Earth and its upper mantle – gathers temporarily in a cistern or 'magma chamber'.

Ash cloud
Clouds of volcanic ash thrown up by the eruption drift long distances from the volcano.

Volcanic bombs
The eruption sends liquid lava spinning into the air. This cools to form heavy boulders that tumble to the ground.

Lava flow
Streams of hot liquid magma – or lava – flow from the volcano's mouth out over the surrounding countryside.

Extinct volcanic pipe
Magma has solidified in the magma chamber and neck of an extinct volcano.

Sedimentary rocks
The magma forces its way through the layer of sedimentary rocks that lies immediately below the Earth's surface.

HOW A VOLCANO WORKS

Deep beneath its surface, the Earth is in motion. Heat from natural radioactivity causes rocks to melt in its interior, and friction generates more heat as the rocks move. The molten rock (called magma) collects in a magma chamber before bursting through at the surface as an erupting volcano.

The shape of the volcano and the degree of violence of the eruptions depend upon the type of lava. Molten mantle tends to be formed where the Earth's crust is pushed apart at mid-ocean ridges, for example, or in the African Rift valley. It consists of runny black basalt that forms gently sloping cones. Molten crust, on the other hand, which is formed at zones where the crust is being pushed together and pressurised, is sticky and forms volcanoes that have steeper slopes.

The explosive mechanism in volcanoes is essentially like that of a champagne bottle popping its cork. Gases and steam build up underneath the sticky lava – sometimes to such an extent that the whole mountain explodes in a massive mushroom cloud of ash and gas. These are the most dangerous and unpredictable, as well as the most common, of the world's 1300 active volcanoes.

Mauna Loa and Hualalai, it is a wide cone, flattened on top, that was formed as the Pacific's ocean floor moved over a hot spot

VOLCANIC INSPIRATION

Tranquil though it may seem today, the English Lake District – famous as the home of the poet William Wordsworth (1770-1850) – was once a string of volcanic islands. A vast eruption some 400 million years ago buried it beneath thick layers of lava and threw up dense clouds of ash that darkened the skies for weeks. Since then, millions of years of accumulating sediment, subterranean movements and erosion have carved the rocky landscape into the beautiful mountain scenery that has inspired so many artists, poets and walkers.

approximately 37 miles (60 km) beneath the Earth's surface where molten rock or magma has collected. Molten basalt forces its way through to the surface in a series of lava flows that build the volcano and pour in sinuous rivers down the mountains. The other Hawaiian islands are extinct volcanoes

on pieces of the Earth's crust that have now moved over and away from the hot spot.

All the Hawaiian islands are made of black basalt, formed in the mantle of the Earth and the commonest type of lava. In a humid climate, basalt weathers quickly, producing the rich soils and lush landscapes typical of these tropical paradises.

Kilauea has been intensively studied, and its eruptions can now be predicted with some accuracy. The first sign of one is a series of earth tremors and a slight swelling of the volcano – measurable only on delicate instruments – as the upper magma chamber fills with molten rock disgorged from below. A few days later, the lava shoots up from the summit in fiery fountains and bursts through fissures on the volcano's flanks.

Frequently, the lava flow disappears underground down a lava tube. These are formed when the top of a flow solidifies, leaving the inside hot enough for the liquid to continue flowing. When the

eruption stops, a long passage remains, which may eventually be colonised by white, cave-dwelling shrimps and spiders.

There are two kinds of solidified basalt on Kilauea, each with its own Hawaiian folkname. *Pahoehoe*, meaning 'ropy', is fluid lava that looks like coiled rope. The second type, found at the ends of lava flows, is *aa* – pronounced 'aah-aah' – which is derived from the cries of those who dare to walk across its sharp, jagged edges.

THE DEVIL'S WATCHTOWER

AN EXTINCT VOLCANO DOMINATES
THE PLAINS OF WYOMING

Surging up from the plains of Wyoming's cattle country, and visible from 100 miles (160 km) away, is Devils Tower, a massive column of rock that was the United States'

BASALT SCULPTURE *Devils Tower in Wyoming once plugged the mouth of a volcano.*

PACIFIC PARADISE *Reefs shelter the coral-built islets of Bora Bora in the South Pacific.*

seven stars of the Pleiades cluster. More recently, in 1977, the tower featured in the film *Close Encounters of the Third Kind* as a landing site for a gigantic space ship.

ISOLATED PARADISE

TRANQUIL ATOLLS LIE WHERE VOLCANIC VIOLENCE ONCE ERUPTED

The Pacific Ocean is littered with isolated and uninhabited coral islands, many of which have been the subject of fantasy and films. But how do these atolls form, given that the Pacific is deep, and coral can grow only in shallow water? The answer is that every coral island marks the site of a vanished volcano.

The pattern is usually the same. The coral first appears as a reef surrounding the cone of a volcano, but movements in

first national monument. At 865 ft (265 m) high, it is an excellent place from which to view five different states: Wyoming, Nebraska, Montana, North Dakota and South Dakota.

This colossal monolith, which looks like a mass of columns clustered together, is in fact the core of an extinct volcano. Fifty million years ago, the rock you see today was molten basalt lava in the pipe of an active volcano, and was surrounded by the sloping layers of ash that formed the cone. As the lava slowly cooled and hardened, shrinkage joints appeared, forming a hexagonal pattern. Then, because the surrounding ash was much softer than the basalt columns, it was eroded away, leaving the breathtaking columns visible for miles around.

The basalt is rich in iron, which gives it a warm, rust-red patina, and the lichens that cover its surface add further colour. All in all, its size and symmetry, and its changing colours as the sunlight plays over it, make the Devils Tower one of the more stunning of the world's natural wonders.

It has always been wreathed in legend. It was known to the indigenous Cheyenne Indians as Bad God's Tower. Another

native American people, the Kiowa, had their own explanation for its existence. A legend tells of seven little girls running from a wild bear. The girls jumped on to a low rock that started to grow higher and higher as the angry bear clawed at it, leaving sharp groove marks behind. The bear finally died of exhaustion, and the girls were immortalised in the heavens as the

CORAL REEFS AND THE ORIGIN OF THE SPECIES

Charles Darwin, founder of the modern theory of evolution, was fascinated by the plant, animal and bird life he found teeming around the myriad coral islands of the Pacific during his famous sea voyage in the *Beagle* (1831–36). He recognised that their isolation provided the ideal environment for the rapid evolution of great numbers of species.

Atolls are a delicate ecosystem; the corals grow, taking nutrients and oxygen from the ocean. More oxygen is generated by algae. Sea urchins and molluscs graze on the coral; worms and shrimps make a home there and are food for other sea creatures. Meanwhile, the top of the reef forms a foothold for coconuts and other seeds carried by the sea; these grow in profusion, fertilised by the lime of the coral sand.

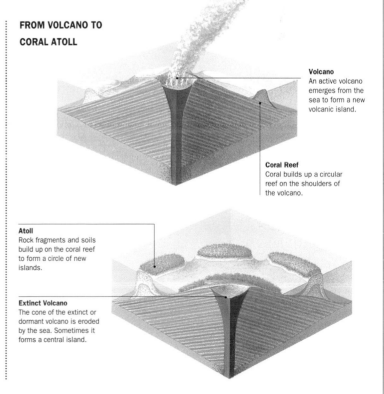

FROM VOLCANO TO CORAL ATOLL

Volcano
An active volcano emerges from the sea to form a new volcanic island.

Coral Reef
Coral builds up a circular reef on the shoulders of the volcano.

Atoll
Rock fragments and soils build up on the coral reef to form a circle of new islands.

Extinct Volcano
The cone of the extinct or dormant volcano is eroded by the sea. Sometimes it forms a central island.

the heart of the Earth cause the volcano to sink. The coral continues to grow, so that the top of the reef stays in sunlight above the surface of the water. Gradually, a circular lagoon appears in the centre of the reef and fills with coral sand. The lower parts of the reef and the deeper layers of the coral sand harden to form a strong limestone base, supporting the living coral above – until, eventually, the crown of the volcano is completely submerged and blanketed in limestone.

The reef, however, continues to grow, creating a circular atoll that encircles a shallow lagoon of coral sand. In this way, the sun-blessed, palm-fringed islets of the South Seas came into being.

SINISTER GIANTS

THE OLGAS: MONSTROUS DOMES AND CUPOLAS IN THE AUSTRALIAN DESERT

In 1872, an Australian explorer, Ernest Giles, noted in his diary that 'the appearance of Mount Olga from this camp is truly wonderful. It displayed to our astonished eyes rounded minarets, giant cupolas and monstrous domes.' He went on to liken these prominences to 'enormous pink haystacks, all leaning against each other'. To the Aboriginal people of Australia, they are simply Kata Tjuta, or 'many heads'.

Mount Olga, 3509 ft (1069 m) high, is part of a group of about 30 dome-shaped peaks lying west of Ayers Rock (Uluru) in Australia's Northern Territory. Known collectively as the Olgas, they are the eroded remains of a long-gone mountain range that was deposited in an ancient sea. There the water separated the material into layers of pebbles and boulders, which finally became cemented together by much finer sand.

Towards the end of the Cambrian Period, about 500 million years ago, these recycled beds of rock were lifted and tilted above sea level. As this happened, the rocks were cracked and weakened, and as

MANY HEADS *Erosion formed the rounded peaks of Australia's Olgas.*

they rose above the sea, erosion attacked them again. Today, all that is left are rounded 'island mountains', called by their German name, inselbergs, by geologists.

The Aboriginals have known about them for some 40 000 years and have used them as sources of fresh water and as places for hunting and shelter. Some of the caves beneath the mountains are decorated with cave paintings that depict events from folklore. One story tells that if tribal laws are broken, a serpent Wanampi will send strong gusts of wind through the gorges between the peaks to remind the people of their duties.

SHAPED BY TIME AND THE ELEMENTS

THE GUILIN HILLS RISE AS SURREAL
LIMESTONE TOWERS IN CHINA'S HEART

Among the world's most magical landscapes are the strange limestone towers that loom above the countryside around Guilin, on the banks of the Li River in southern China. Generations of artists and poets have been inspired by Guilin's dreamlike landscape – turquoise clusters of conical hills, sometimes wreathed in mist except where a thicket of trees or shrubs appears high up as if floating in mid-air. Similar formations jut from Along Bay on the Vietnamese side of the Gulf of Tonkin.

Pillars of limestone rock sculpted by the wind, chemical erosion and rainwater are not uncommon. What makes the towers of Guilin unique is their exceptional height – the tallest rises 400 ft (120 m) from the green paddy fields beneath.

The story begins some 300 million years ago, in Earth's Carboniferous Age. Most limestone consists of many layers of calcified skeletons accumulating on the sea bed – billions of tiny sea organisms gradually being compressed to become sediment and finally rock. In the Carboniferous Age, the Guilin region was an unusually thick layer of sediment lying beneath an ancient sea. Geological movements later raised it above sea level, where it was exposed to the effects of erosion. Limestone is easily eroded: as rainwater collects carbon dioxide from the air or from the soil, it becomes carbonic acid, a solution strong enough to dissolve a calcium compound.

Limestone scenery tends to look bare and dry on the surface, since the water flows beneath the ground, enlarging fissures and crevices, and carving out hollows and sculptural shapes. The result is a 'karst' – a type of landscape named after an area in former Yugoslavia that has a notable example of it. In the Guilin region, the raised limestone was worn fairly flat, except where water cut out a network of valleys and opened up caverns and waterways below ground level.

Later geological movements raised the area once again, and the process of erosion continued, sparing some of the more resistant limestone masses, but wearing away the roofs of hollow spaces underground and cutting deeper, wider valleys until the water table reached its present level. By then, all that remained of what had been a vast limestone plateau were these tall narrow towers.

Today, it is the water around the bottom of these towers that has the greatest effect in shaping the landscape. In Along Bay it gnaws into the rock, moved by the tides and

LIMESTONE TOWERS *Earth movements raised the 'towers' of Guilin in China (left) and Along Bay in Vietnam (above).*

currents. In the Guilin region the water acids, produced by decomposing plant material in an area of intensive cultivation, also accelerate erosion. The towers are less affected by the forces of wind, rain and erosion at their tops than at the bottom, and in time may well become narrower.

WHERE AN ANCIENT ROLLING BOULDER STOPPED

GROOVE MARKS CREATE A PUZZLE IN AMERICA'S DEATH VALLEY DESERT

Death Valley in California is the hottest, driest and lowest place in North America. This inhospitable environment contains an enigma – a series of grooves that cross part of its sun-baked surface, each brought to an abrupt halt by a large boulder.

Some 50 million years ago, forces deep inside the Earth built the high mountain ranges – notably the Rockies – on America's West Coast. East of the mountains, a series of faults developed, and some blocks of land between them sank to form rift valleys, while neighbouring blocks were thrust upwards to form more mountains.

Rain is rare in these lands. Warm winds carrying moist air from the Pacific are deflected up over the Sierra Nevada, where the moisture condenses and falls as rain. As the wind reaches the other side, it is practically devoid of moisture and desert conditions prevail. Nevertheless, there is plenty of evidence of water at work. When rare

POWER TO CUT *Water that once ran along Australia's Finke River carved a gorge through the Macdonnell Range.*

rains do fall, they arrive as a deluge. With no exit to the sea, the water accumulates on the valley floors, forming temporary lakes that eventually dry in the sun, leaving layers of salt and hard-baked mud. These dried-up lake beds are called 'playas'.

The oval-shaped Racetrack Playa may have been been made by fierce winds blowing boulders along the surface after rain, when the lake bed was wet and slippery, or during rare winter frosts. Alternatively, the rocks may have been carried in blocks of ice that were beginning to thaw.

IT ONLY FLOWS WHEN IT POURS

CENTRAL AUSTRALIA'S FINKE RIVER FLOWS ONLY AFTER HEAVY RAINS

The Finke River rises just west of the town of Alice Springs, in the mountains of Central Australia's Macdonnell Ranges. It then flows for 993 miles (1600 km) south-

eastwards towards Lake Eyre – or at least it does sometimes. For the Finke River is an intermittent river that flows only after heavy rain. In good years, the Finke Valley has about 14 in (25 cm) of rain, but many years pass without any rain at all – until, suddenly, a torrential storm provides enough water for several years to come.

The air is so dry that any rain rapidly evaporates, usually long before it has time to soak into the ground. Once there must have been a good deal more rain, because the river has cut a deep gorge through the Macdonnell Ranges. However, as it reaches the lowland area south of the mountains, its course almost vanishes. Instead of a clear river bed, it wanders around the river basin, living up to its Aboriginal name of Larapinta, the Snake.

From the air, the whole basin looks arid, the Sun reflecting off the white salt pans and accentuating the glaring red of the clay pans. In the occasional wet years the Finke reaches Lake Eyre, a vast, shallow, salty lake that has no outlet to the sea. A centre of inland drainage, the lake is getting saltier all the time as its meagre water content evaporates.

ICE ON THE MOVE

Glaciers form in cold mountain regions where more snow falls than melts. Although made only of compressed ice crystals, glaciers and their cargo of rocky debris gouge out broad valleys and slice their way through mountainsides.

Many powerful forces have shaped the landscapes people live in – and one of the most dramatic of them all is the force of frozen water. The Alps and Himalayas, the Rockies and England's Lake District, the mountains and fjords of Norway – over the last million years or so, much of Earth's most spectacular scenery has been carved, eroded, scraped and shaped by moving ice. For despite its appearance, ice is not rigid. Under pressure it will deform and move – the characteristic that has made it so powerful.

During the Pleistocene Age, which ended about 10 000 years ago, there were several ice ages when the climate of the world was much colder than it is today. The ice caps around the poles thickened with extra snowfall and spread outwards, and glaciers in the high mountain ranges expanded down the valleys like solid rivers. As the climate worsened at the beginning of each ice age, the falling snow accumulated until huge volumes of it were pressing down on the layers beneath. Like a snowball pressed between the hands, these lower layers gradually turned to ice.

At the point where the ice is in contact with the rock, the pressure is so high that it turns the ice into water, creating a thin layer of liquid that acts as a lubricant, allowing the ice to slide over the rock beneath it. Sometimes, the movement is so slow, perhaps a couple of yards a year, that it can only be measured over long periods.

At other times, glaciers surge forward by several yards a day, particularly during warm periods.

Where a continental ice sheet or a glacier flows over a steep rock slope, an ice fall may well develop. The ice's surface becomes broken and cracked – crevassed – as it stretches to follow the slope of the rock underneath. One of the most famous ice falls, in Mount Everest's Western cirque, lies on the route taken by Hillary and Tenzing on the first successful ascent of the world's highest mountain in 1953. Many climbers claim that the ice can be heard moving as they scale the world's great mountain ranges

FROM THE PEAKS TO THE PLAINS

ICE POWER *Glaciers like this shaped modern Alaska.*

PERPETUAL MOTION *The grinding of glaciers is one of the most spectacular ways in which rocks are moved from the peaks to the plains.*

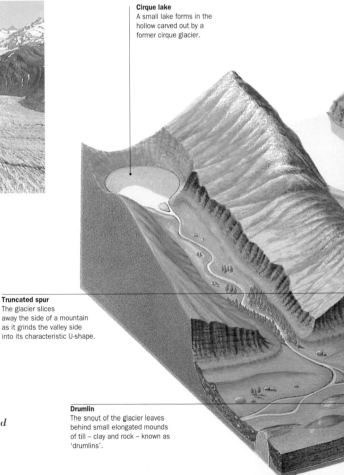

Cirque lake
A small lake forms in the hollow carved out by a former cirque glacier.

Truncated spur
The glacier slices away the side of a mountain as it grinds the valley side into its characteristic U-shape.

Drumlin
The snout of the glacier leaves behind small elongated mounds of till – clay and rock – known as 'drumlins'.

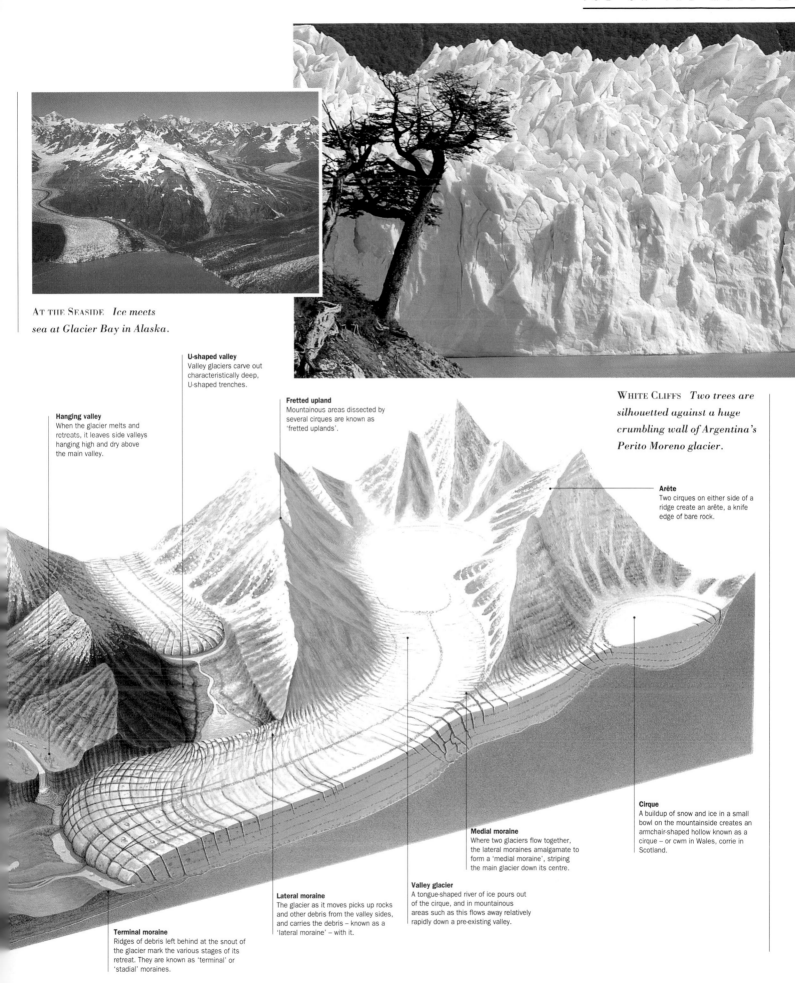

AT THE SEASIDE *Ice meets sea at Glacier Bay in Alaska.*

U-shaped valley
Valley glaciers carve out characteristically deep, U-shaped trenches.

Fretted upland
Mountainous areas dissected by several cirques are known as 'fretted uplands'.

WHITE CLIFFS *Two trees are silhouetted against a huge crumbling wall of Argentina's Perito Moreno glacier.*

Hanging valley
When the glacier melts and retreats, it leaves side valleys hanging high and dry above the main valley.

Arête
Two cirques on either side of a ridge create an arête, a knife edge of bare rock.

Cirque
A buildup of snow and ice in a small bowl on the mountainside creates an armchair-shaped hollow known as a cirque – or cwm in Wales, corrie in Scotland.

Medial moraine
Where two glaciers flow together, the lateral moraines amalgamate to form a 'medial moraine', striping the main glacier down its centre.

Valley glacier
A tongue-shaped river of ice pours out of the cirque, and in mountainous areas such as this flows away relatively rapidly down a pre-existing valley.

Lateral moraine
The glacier as it moves picks up rocks and other debris from the valley sides, and carries the debris – known as a 'lateral moraine' – with it.

Terminal moraine
Ridges of debris left behind at the snout of the glacier mark the various stages of its retreat. They are known as 'terminal' or 'stadial' moraines.

and avalanches can be heard in summer as the ice weakens in the heat.

Ice flowing down a valley behaves in much the same way as water in a river, which tends to flow slowly near the banks and more quickly in the middle. The ice in contact with the valley walls is slowed by friction, while the ice in the centre of the glacier flows more freely and therefore faster, with cracks and crevasses developing in it as a result. The crevasses start near the edges and curve upstream towards the middle of the glacier. They are often visible from the air, but at surface level, especially after heavy snowfalls, they can be hidden by snow bridges. In the massive ice fields of Antarctica and Greenland, crevasses may be hundreds of yards deep.

In both places, the dome-shaped ice sheets covering them are huge. The ice in Greenland rises in places to over 10 000 ft (3000 m) above sea level. In the Antarctic, meanwhile, it has been estimated that 7.1 million cu miles (30 million km^3) of ice covers an area of 5.3 million sq miles (13.8 million km^2). Its weight is so great that it pushes the land down below sea level, and it extends out beyond the coast as ice shelves. Isolated mountains, known by the Eskimo word nunataks, poke through the vast ice desert like islands in a pure white sea.

During the last Ice Age, about 30 per cent of the world's land surface was covered by ice, but today about 11 per cent is buried, locking up three-quarters of the world's fresh water. There is no shortage of water in the world – it is just in the wrong place and in the deep-freeze. If all the ice melted, the world's sea level would rise by about 300 ft (90 m).

ICE'S MOUNTAIN ARMCHAIRS

CIRQUES, CWMS, CORRIES – DIFFERENT NAMES FOR ICE-CARVED AMPHITHEATRES

Huge armchair-shaped hollows in the mountains are a legacy of the ice sheets that covered large areas of the Earth during the last great Ice Age, ending some 10 000 years ago. Known variously as cirques (in France), cwms (in Wales) or corries (in Scotland), they are a feature of many mountainous areas, such as the Black Mountains in central Wales and the Pyrenees. Several of them grouped together result in a 'fretted upland' of sharp-edged ridges (or cols) and rounded, steep-sided hollows often containing small lakes.

One of the most impressive of cirques is the huge Cirque de Gavarnie in the Pyrenees, shaped like an ancient amphitheatre. Its surrounding walls rise between 1640 and 2300 ft (500 and 700 m) from the floor of the cirque, and the distance around its semicircular base is over 2 miles (3.2 km). It also has a waterfall that plunges 1385 ft (422 m) in a single leap. Another spectacular example of a cirque faces out towards the sea near Adalvik in north-western Iceland, where

CARVED BY ICE *Bare slopes plunge dramatically around a cirque in the Black Mountains of central Wales.*

snow-dusted slopes rise majestically on three sides, with the front open to the icy expanses of the Greenland Sea.

Once there was no more than a small stream flowing through the site of such cirques. The stream rose in the mountains and cut its own valley down to the plains and finally the sea. Then came a colder age. Snow slid down from the surrounding peaks, piling up in the valley below. As more and more snow accumulated, its weight eventually compacted it into ice. The newborn glacier began to spread, filling every crack and fissure in the rocks, freezing and splitting them, and tearing away great chunks of the rock face. The glacier – by now a mass weighing thousands of tons – continued its relentless progress, constantly exerting its pressure forwards and downwards.

As snow cascaded from the mountaintops, it brought with it a freight of rocks and boulders, all tearing at the ground beneath. And as the slope became more and more acute, the height of the snow increased, allowing still more snow to be packed into the emerging hollows on the mountainside. Hence, the glacier increased in weight and strength. The cirques owe their bowl-like shape, which was revealed in the mountainside when the glacier finally melted, to this series of events.

TENAYA CREEK: AN ICE AGE LEGACY

A CANYON-LIKE VALLEY SCULPTED

BY A MONUMENTAL GLACIER

Lean out and shout across the sheer 765 yd (700 m) chasm of Tenaya Creek slicing through California's Yosemite National Parkland and you get a perfect echo from the distant cliff faces.

Only ice could have gouged this monumental valley through the mountains – an awe-inspiring legacy of glacial action that occurred about 150 000 years ago. The Yosemite region lies on the same latitude as San Francisco, where there is little ice nowadays except on the topmost peaks of the Sierra Nevada mountains, rising inland on the other side of the Sacramento Valley. But once the whole area was blanketed with thick glaciers. From

STANDING ON RISING GROUND

Parts of Scandinavia, the northern British Isles and North America are still rising at a rate of between $2/5$ and 40 in (1 and 100 cm) per century. When the great ice sheets of the ice ages melted, land that had previously been buried beneath the ice, and weighted down by it so that it lay below the level of the sea, began to rise again. Even though the last Ice Age ended 10 000 years ago, the process has continued, and some of the land is still rising. Geologists estimate that the floor of the northern Baltic Sea, for example, could rise anything up to 330 ft (100 m) before the movement stops.

these, huge sheets of ice moved down into old river valleys, scoring and carving through them to change the landscape. In the case of Tenaya Creek, they left an existing river valley considerably deeper

FROM GLACIER TO THE SEA: HOW ICEBERGS FORM

Around Antarctica, Greenland, the Canadian Arctic and along the shores of Alaska are the points where glaciers and ice sheets reach the sea. And since ice is less dense than sea water, they float.

The zone where ice and sea meet is very turbulent. Storm waves attack the ice, and the warmer sea water softens it. Every day the tides flex and weaken it until huge lumps fall off and float away as icebergs. In the North Atlantic and Pacific, most come from broken valley glaciers and are jagged and irregular, like the one the *Titanic* struck in 1912. In the southern oceans, they come from the vast ice sheets of Antarctica and tend to be massive with flat tops: the biggest are as large as the Isle of Wight off southern England or Barbados in the West Indies. Drifting around the sea for years on end, these floating white castles are deceptive, since seven-eighths of them lies beneath the surface. As the ice melts, fresh water runs off and mixes with the sea water. The heavier fresh water empties into the salt water, drawing up currents rich in nutrients. Here ice shrimps crowd the less saline water, while seals and sea birds pick off feeding fish. Eventually, the bottom of the iceberg is eroded; it becomes top-heavy and flips over.

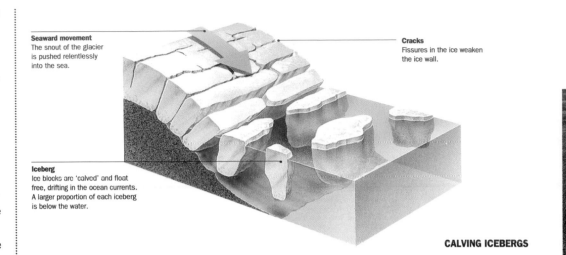

Seaward movement
The snout of the glacier is pushed relentlessly into the sea.

Cracks
Fissures in the ice weaken the ice wall.

Iceberg
Ice blocks are 'calved' and float free, drifting in the ocean currents. A larger proportion of each iceberg is below the water.

CALVING ICEBERGS

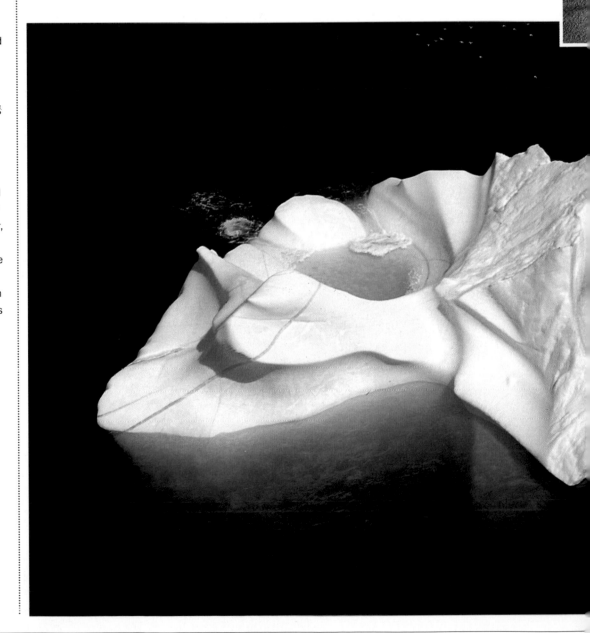

CASTLE IN ICE *An Arctic iceberg glows ghostly white in darkened seas off Greenland. The bulk of such bergs lies underneath the water.*

CRACKED SHEET *An Antarctic ice sheet fragments where it meets the slightly warmer sea.*

than it had been before and up to 1640 ft (500m) wider.

Although it looks like a canyon (strictly, a gorge formed by a river), Tenaya Creek is a glacial trough that preserves the U-shape of such valleys long after the ice that created it melted. Ancient glacial scars like this survive all over the world, from the Rockies to the Andes, the Alps to the Himalayas. Cutting through numerous mountain ranges, they have left rocky highways that enable modern travellers and tourists to penetrate the foothills and approach the highest peaks.

SILENT GRANDEUR

MILFORD SOUND: CROWNING GLORY OF NEW ZEALAND'S FJORDLAND

Milford Sound lies on the south-west coast of New Zealand's South Island. Breakers travelling from Antarctica batter the coastline to form sheer cliff faces that rise 328 yd (300 m) high. In places, the sea cuts deep inlets, like narrow knife wounds, the longest of which is Milford Sound, 2 miles (3 km) wide and reaching 12 miles (19 km) inland. Rising above are the tall,

jagged outlines of mountains reminiscent of the Alps or Himalayas. In fact, it was here that the New Zealander Sir Edmund Hillary trained for his conquest of Everest in 1953.

Among these mountains, Mitre Peak was given its name in 1851 by a British naval officer, Captain John Lort Stokes, because it resembles a bishop's mitre; it rises straight from the water to soar over 5550 ft (1690 m) high. A few miles inland, the permanently snow-clad Tutoko Peak rises to a height of 9042 ft (2756 m). The Sutherland Falls, named after an early settler in the area, cascade down nearly 2000 ft (610 m). The landscape with cliffs plunging sheer into the waters evokes the fjords of Scandinavia – this kind of inlet is known in New Zealand as a 'sound'.

The landscape is a combination of two distinct geological forms – those that are also characteristic of the Alps, and those characteristic of the coasts of Scandinavia. Powerful glaciers gouged through the

TWO AGES OF ICE *Snowy peaks loom over the ancient glacial valley of Milford Sound in New Zealand's South Island.*

FOOTPRINTS OF THE GLACIER *Lakes in the Canadian Arctic fill shallow depressions left by ancient ice sheets moving across areas of open country.*

mountains during one ice age, and then, in a later one, they dug even deeper into the old glacial valleys. When the ice melted, the seas rose and carved the coastline into cliffs, sometimes penetrating deep into the U-shaped troughs the glaciers had left behind them.

MOSAIC LAKES IN CANADA AND FINLAND

LAKES FORMED WHERE ICE SHEETS
CROSSED A PLAIN

Canada has more than 2 million lakes, more than any other country in the world. Finland, a much smaller land, has almost as many, but hers are more densely packed. In parts of both countries, the lakes are huddled together so closely that they cover more than nine-tenths of the surface area and are separated only by narrow strips of shingle. From a small seaplane – the only

practical means of transport in areas like this – the impression is of some giant aquatic mosaic.

The lakes lie in long parallel lines, either straight or gently curving, and form designs that can be decoded only from a considerable distance – from an aircraft, say, or outer space – when two key elements emerge. First, the lakes reflect the geological structure of the area: they follow the lines of the region's different kinds of rock. Most of the Canadian Shield, for example, is less than 2000 ft (600 m) above sea level, its monotonous landscape etched into ancient, folded rocks. Finland's lakes are sculpted from a huge granite shield that was formed in the Precambrian era about 500 million years ago.

Second, they look like the work of a giant rasp that has swept across whole regions, leaving teeth marks deeply impressed in places, with waste left behind as heaps and ridges. In both Canada and Finland, the mosaic lakelands occur only in regions where the land was long ago worn almost flat by ice and running water. Here, the ice sheets that covered the land

did not encounter any resistant hills and mountains in their path as they did elsewhere in the world. Instead, they travelled smoothly in a single blanket of ice across gentle slopes, for there were few valleys for them to probe. The rasp marks were dug out by the rocky debris they carried.

ANCIENT HITCHHIKERS IN AN ALIEN LAND

ERRATICS – ROCKS AND BOULDERS
ABANDONED BY MELTED GLACIERS

Erratics are rocks that have strayed a long way from their original source: for example, a rock isolated in an area that is otherwise bereft of stones, and different in its mineral content from the surrounding strata. Erratics have been carried, pushed and dragged by a glacier before being dumped – the heaviest rocks first – as soon as the melting glacier was no longer strong enough to transport them.

Some erratics can be traced back to their source across great distances – 600 miles (around 1000 km) is not unusual – and the largest may weigh 1000 tons. There

HOW 'ERRATICS' WERE LEFT BEHIND

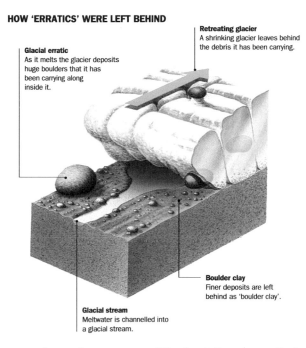

Glacial erratic
As it melts the glacier deposits huge boulders that it has been carrying along inside it.

Retreating glacier
A shrinking glacier leaves behind the debris it has been carrying.

Boulder clay
Finer deposits are left behind as 'boulder clay'.

Glacial stream
Meltwater is channelled into a glacial stream.

are rocks on the east coast of England, for example, that originally came from the region around Oslo in Norway.

However, although the sight of a block of alien granite squatting on a sandstone hilltop is impressive, it was just part of the glacier's freight. The bulk consisted of smaller lumps of rock, loose stones, gravel and sand – materials known to geologists as 'till' – that the glacier itself helped to create by its crushing and abrading action. When the glacier melted, most of this cargo was discarded in the form of enormous piles of debris (moraines), appearing as horseshoe-shaped deposits at the front of the glacier, or as ridges to either side of its tongue. Sometimes it was left beneath the ice as long thin 'flutes', often miles long, extending in the direction of the glacier's movement.

Each pebble and every grain of sand in these glacial waste dumps is as much an 'erratic' as the occasional huge and impressive boulder left high and dry in gently rolling countryside.

PREHISTORIC TRACKS OF AN ICY MONSTER

THE TELLTALE SCORE MARKS LEFT BY A PASSING GLACIER

The deep grooves in the rock on the island of Spitsbergen in the Arctic look as if they were made by a monster's claws. They also sink to record depths. Known as 'striations',

WANDERERS Melting Ice Age glaciers deposited boulders thousands of miles from their original homes (left). Some 'erratics' (above) were left behind as far south as Arizona.

they are, in fact, the tracks left by massive glaciers. They are not the work of the ice itself scoring the surface of the rock, but were rasped out by the baggage of boulders and rocky fragments that a moving glacier picks up in its underside. As a result, the glacier acts rather like a sheet of coarse sandpaper. In Spitsbergen's case, the glacier was at least 7000 ft (2135 m) thick, its weight bearing down with a pressure at ground level 36 times greater than that exerted by the Great Pyramid of Cheops on its foundations.

Only the hardest of rocks bear the marks of such striations; on softer ones, they would have been erased by the next glacier. Although the glacier generally moved in a straight line, it also rose and fell and swayed from side to side, rather like a liner ploughing through high seas. This and the time of the year – and hence the amount of ice – account for the varied depths and shapes of the striations.

Striations also occur on stones and small boulders embedded in another rock known as 'tillite'. This is made from rounded fragments of glacial rubble – 'till' – that is cemented together with finely ground glacial debris known as 'rock flour'.

CLAW MARKS Rocks trapped in a glacier's underside gouged these grooves into the rock beneath.

THE POWER
OF WATER

Soft rocks let water through – hard rocks are more of an obstacle. In its journey from rainfall to rivers to the sea, water sculpts the landscape, creating features that range from spectacular waterfalls to intricate cave systems.

Earth is the only planet in the solar system known for certain to have water on its surface. Indeed, life itself developed in the water nearly 4 billion years ago, and ever since water has been sculpting the continents.

The first oceans were formed from water vapour, released with other gases from the young Earth's seething interior. As the planet's crust cooled, the vapour condensed to create the first oceans. The Sun, however, was also at work, warming the oceans' surface, which caused some water to evaporate again. This vapour condensed to form clouds. The water droplets in the clouds fell as rain, back into the oceans, or onto the continents, where some of it collected into channels and rivers. Under the influence of gravity, the water was then carried back to the sea.

Rivers are major shapers of the landscape. In their upper reaches, they flow fast, cutting deep V-shaped valleys. Rocks, soil and debris are washed in by rain, or torn from the banks by the force of the water. The river carries this load on its journey to the sea. After a storm or a flood, it can carry a huge amount of sediment, which may explain the biblical story of the Nile turning to blood (probably red desert silt washed into the river in a sudden storm upstream).

As a river broadens in its lower reaches, the gradient of the bed becomes less steep and the torrent slower, and the heavier sediment settles on the bottom. Fed by tributaries, the river continues to expand, and the course of its meanderings cuts away at the high ground, widening the valley and smoothing out a broad flood plain. Some sediment is deposited as mudbanks or a delta, or swept out to sea where it

THE RIVER'S SEAWARD JOURNEY

Source
Run-off from mountain streams, glaciers or lakes provides the source of a river.

Headwaters
Several streams and sources of water form the 'headwaters' which converge into a single river.

Waterfall
The river erodes soft rock more rapidly than hard rock. A shelf forms the water flows over it as a waterfall.

Oxbow lake
Sometimes a meandering river takes a short-cut at a bend. A small isolated 'oxbow' lake forms at the side of the river.

Meanders
As a river reaches flatter ground and its pace slackens, it tends to curve back and forth across the broad valley floor.

Flood Plain
The land on either side of the river is liable to flooding when the river overflows its banks.

Gorge
The river cuts deeply into the rock to form a steep-sided gorge or canyon.

Swallow hole
In limestone country, a river sometimes disappears below ground.

Spring
An underground river or stream reappears at the surface.

FACE TO FACE *Rainbows form between the twin faces of the Iguaçu Falls.*

eventually sinks in layers, gradually hardening to form the rocks of the future.

In limestone areas, streams and rivers may disappear down a hole and run underground for considerable distances. Limestone is soluble, and over the years the running water hollows out cave systems. Some lime is redeposited, either to form travertine – a kind of limestone often used for the facings of buildings – or to create hanging stalactites or standing stalagmites.

The sea is another powerful shaper of the landscape. The waves can act as a sculptor, tearing rocks from cliffs, or as a potter, laying down new sediment in the form of beaches and sand spits. They smash against cliffs, eroding the softer rocks or strata and forming caves. Sometimes these break through to form sea arches. Eventually they may collapse to leave isolated stacks, such as

DOWN THE STREAM *A river wends its way from bubbling stream to broad sea delta.*

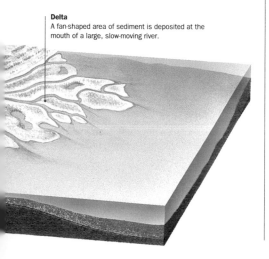

Delta
A fan-shaped area of sediment is deposited at the mouth of a large, slow-moving river.

the Needles off the Isle of Wight in the English Channel.

Changes in sea level affect coastal landscapes. Where it has fallen, raised beaches are left high and dry as terraces. Where it has risen, the mouths of valleys are inundated, forming deep natural harbours, such as the fjords of Norway.

AN OCEAN POURING INTO AN ABYSS

CASCADING WATERFALLS OFFER SOME OF NATURE'S MOST AWESOME SIGHTS

Three of the world's most spectacular waterfalls are the Angel Falls, the Iguaçu Falls and the Victoria Falls. The Angel Falls in Venezuela are on a tributary of the Orinoco, tumbling 3212 ft (979 m) in all – with a plummet of 2648 ft (807 m) in a single sheer drop. On the border between Brazil and Argentina, the Iguaçu Falls send up to 48 000 tons of water per second cascading 279 ft (85 m) down from the Paraná Plateau. And where Zambia meets Zimbabwe, the Victoria Falls are a wall of water over 5250 ft (1600 m) wide, roaring more than 330 ft (100 m) down into a narrow gorge.

A waterfall's sheet or jet of water hardly touches the rock during its vertical plunge. Cascading clear of the face, it thrusts outward from above with all the momentum of its horizontal speed. As a result, the cliff face escapes direct erosion, even if the flow is enormous: it is even possible sometimes to stay dry behind a curtain of water at the foot of a fall. The colossal weight of the water does, however, dig a deep vertical trench at the base. This tends to expand both downstream with the flow of the water, and upstream, where the falling water undercuts the cliff face, creating an overhang that may collapse in large slabs.

Nesting and roosting amongst the rocks and crevices behind the Iguaçu Falls are dusky swifts. Here they are safe from any predators such as ocelots (forest-dwelling cats) and raccoon-like coatimundis, which prefer not to approach the 2^1/$_2$ mile (4 km) wide cascade of plunging water.

CANYON GRANDEUR IN UTAH'S PARKLANDS

SANDSTONE CARVINGS AND POLISHED
PEBBLES WHERE TWO RIVERS MEET

Stretching out where the Colorado River meets the Green River in the western United States, Canyonlands National Park of Utah covers 527 sq miles (1365 km^2). It consists of an immense wilderness area of high sandstone cliffs, flat-topped buttes (abruptly rising hills) and mesas (whose summits are less than 1 sq mile in area). There are stone spires and towers, arches,

---

WHERE THE COLORADO RIVER SLICED DEEP

The deepest scar in Earth's surface is the Grand Canyon in north-west Arizona. It is 6500 ft (2000 m) deep, about 18 miles (29 km) wide at its broadest point and 280 miles (450 km) long. It was formed as the Colorado River sliced deeply into the Colorado Plateau, a process that started about 10 million years ago. The horizontal rock strata exposed in the canyon's sides – yellow limestones, grey-blue limestones, white and brown sandstones, pink granites, and black flaky schists – are a visual history of the Earth, dating back 2000 million years.

---

balanced rocks and awesomely deep, steep-sided canyons.

The area is the product of several forces. The first is the gradual rise of the entire surrounding region, which for 60 million years has been steadily pushed up

GIANT HORSESHOE *River action has carved a brick-red horseshoe canyon in the Utah wilderness.*

by the uplifting of the nearby Rocky Mountain chain – itself the product of a collision between two continental plates.

The second is water erosion that sliced into the various horizontal beds of rock to form flat tablelands separated by deep canyons, or carved out isolated mesas and smaller, tower-like remnants or buttes. The mesas occur where a capping of hard rocks has resisted erosion and protected the softer rocks beneath them. Continued erosion to the sides of the mesa may turn it into a butte or may lead to the formation of a separate butte rising close to the main body of the mesa.

The wind also carries sand at or near ground level and so larger rocks are sometimes worn away faster at their base, leaving huge, flattened boulders perched precariously on narrow necks. The third force is, in fact, such sand-laden winds, which scour the surviving features to form all manner of strange geological shapes, sandblasting boulders and pebbles until they are polished and smooth.

POTHOLES DRILLED BY SWIRLING WATERS

THE WORK OF MANY MILLENNIA BROUGHT
LUCK TO TRANSVAAL'S FARMER BOURKE

Water always finds its own level, kept on the move by a combination of gravity and atmospheric pressure. When it is forced by some obstacle to take a sudden change of direction, it can set up a circular current with the energy of a whirlpool.

If in the process a hard rock, such as granite, is picked up by the swirling water, it is thrown around, scouring into the softer sandstone beneath until, after several millennia, it leaves a large bowl-shaped depression. The most spectacular of these bowls are known as 'giant's kettles' – deep cylindrical pot-holes up to 20 ft (6 m) deep. They have the advantage that they conserve water in times of drought, attracting both humans and other animals.

A group of 'kettles', known as Bourke's Luck Potholes, lies in the Transvaal of South Africa. It was prospectors panning for gold upstream from property belonging to a farmer called Tom Bourke who inspired him to search the bottom of his potholes for nuggets that might have been washed down from their labours. His hunch proved correct: he found gold, and the holes were forever after known as Bourke's Luck.

GORGES AND TOWERING CLIFFS

COLLAPSING LIMESTONE CAVES REVEAL
THE DRAMA OF A GORGE

Canyons, gullies, ravines and gorges are mostly formed in one of two ways: a river flowing over a cliff or hard rock ledge and eroding it; or a river flowing underground in limestone country and forming a cave system. In the latter case, the roof of the cave system eventually collapses and opens the steep-sided channel – the new gorge – to the sky.

In Britain, the best-known gorges are those cut in the limestone rock at Cheddar in Somerset, at Gordale in the Yorkshire Dales and near Castleton in Derbyshire, where there are a number of steep-sided narrow valleys.

Some of the vast gorges in other parts of the world were cut by rivers. In China, the Chang Jiang, or Yangtse Kiang, has carved the Three Gorges, which run for nearly 124 miles (200 km) through the mountainous rim of Sichuan province. These were probably formed as the Chang Jiang eroded its channel downwards at the same time as the mountains to the east of Sichuan were folded upwards. The river is 330 ft (100 m) wide in places, and travellers drifting down it or fighting upstream against the currents, stare up at 3900 ft (1200 m) limestone cliffs. It is scarcely surprising that the chill of night lingers on the water long after the mountaintops are in full sunlight.

Another spectacular gorge is that cut by the Niagara River – flowing from Lake Erie to Lake Ontario on the US-Canadian border – below the Niagara Falls. The gorge at Niagara is recent in geological terms – a mere 12 500 years old. At the end of the last Ice Age, Lake Erie was much larger than it is now, filled with water from the melting ice fields. Lake Erie overflowed the limestone of the Niagara escarpment and ran into what is now Lake Ontario. The hard limestone of the escarpment is underlain by soft shale rock. As the water thundered over the falls, the soft shale was eroded away and huge blocks of limestone were unloosed, crashing into the river bed and creating a narrow, steep-sided channel, the Niagara Gorge of today.

It is still forming, as the Niagara Falls themselves are continuously being cut back by the power of the falling water and retreat upstream.

HOT SPRINGS AT YELLOWSTONE PARK

WHERE STEAMING SPRINGS CREATE A
FANTASY OF LIMESTONE TERRACES

Crystallised minerals appear whenever sea or lake water evaporates. The Dead Sea, for example, is a gigantic evaporation dish, powered by the heat of the Sun. A similar – albeit slower – process occurs when water gradually seeps through underground limestone rocks to build up stalactites and stalagmites. Other natural processes daub minerals over whole mountainsides in spectacular washes of white and yellow, or mould minerals into impressive tiers of delicately scalloped bowls, frozen torrents and natural dams.

Sometimes the resulting shapes look as if they had been designed by some fantastic sculptor-architect working on a superhuman scale. In Yellowstone Park, the spectacular terraced pools at Mammoth Hot Springs bear the name of 'Minerva Terraces' and look as if only a goddess could have made them. For more than 2000 years, some equally exuberant formations in eastern Turkey have drawn visitors to Pamukkale, whose name means 'cotton castle'. Then there is the stairway of blue,

WATER AND ROCK *Boulders driven by swirling water bored the potholes at Bourke's Luck in the Transvaal of South Africa.*

The hydrothermal springs on the high plateau at Pamukkale in Turkey are fed by rainwater that has seeped through layers of limestone. The springs deposit their load of limestone downhill as dazzling white gours that form ramparts jutting 295 ft (90 m) from the mountainside. Where the

MINERAL SCULPTURES *Stalactites and stalagmites form in caves where water seeps through limestone.*

CARVED IN LIMESTONE *Brilliant blue waters flow between the cliffs of Katherine Gorge in north Australia.*

green and turquoise lakes at Band-i-Amir in Afghanistan: an oasis of beauty in the heart of an almost inaccessible wilderness.

The Yellowstone area is crammed with volcanic geysers that sporadically spout jets of sparkling hot water laden with mineral salts leached from the rocks. Old Faithful, the most celebrated of its geysers, erupts 200 ft (60 m) high, a boiling waterspout.

Sometimes, the water creates basins, where it deposits salts as layers of crystals that grow at a faster rate where the water is shallowest – at the downhill edge of the basin. Gradually a dam (or 'gour') builds up; here, the dominant colour is the sulphur yellow coming from the volcanic rock below, giving the park its name. Depending on the temperature, other rocks are dissolved as well, leaving their traces in the multi-coloured layers. Every day, for example, an extra two tons of limestone are added to the Minerva Terraces at Mammoth Hot Springs.

WHAT MAKES A GORGE

Limestone country is best for gorges. Here, river water, which changes into very weak carbonic acid by absorbing carbon dioxide from the soil and atmosphere, seeps through the rock, eating it away. First, it creates small cracks and fissures, in a tracery of vertical and horizontal lines. It then enlarges them to form wide shafts or potholes and caves. Streams and rivers disappear down vertical shafts and flow underground in complex cave systems. If a cave roof becomes too thin, it collapses and a gorge is formed. Gorges are also created when rivers slice down deeply and almost vertically through limestone rocks.

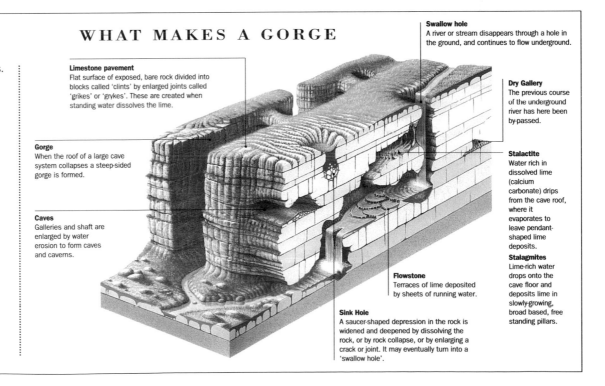

Swallow hole
A river or stream disappears through a hole in the ground, and continues to flow underground.

Limestone pavement
Flat surface of exposed, bare rock divided into blocks called 'clints' by enlarged joints called 'grikes' or 'grykes'. These are created when standing water dissolves the lime.

Gorge
When the roof of a large cave system collapses a steep-sided gorge is formed.

Caves
Galleries and shaft are enlarged by water erosion to form caves and caverns.

Dry Gallery
The previous course of the underground river has here been by-passed.

Stalactite
Water rich in dissolved lime (calcium carbonate) drips from the cave roof, where it evaporates to leave pendant-shaped lime deposits.

Stalagmites
Lime-rich water drops onto the cave floor and deposits lime in slowly-growing, broad based, free standing pillars.

Flowstone
Terraces of lime deposited by sheets of running water.

Sink Hole
A saucer-shaped depression in the rock is widened and deepened by dissolving the rock, or by rock collapse, or by enlarging a crack or joint. It may eventually turn into a 'swallow hole'.

CHANNELLED VIOLENCE *Superheated water spouts into the air as geysers in Yellowstone Park.*

ground is flatter, walls and terraces enclose warm pools of mineral-rich spring water where visitors bathe for sheer pleasure, as well as for their reputed healing powers.

In Band-i-Amir in Afghanistan the walls are as high as 130 ft (40 m) – strong enough to confine a series of six large lakes whose beds are coated with mineral deposits. Most of the water here comes from the streams and glaciers above and is therefore cold. The chief builders are microscopic algae, which precipitate mineral salts by absorbing carbon dioxide from the water.

KINGLY DELTA

RIVERS CARRY THEIR SILT TO THE SEA AND LEAVE A DELTA

The vast mud flats of river estuaries along the Kimberley coast of north-western Australia form a constantly changing landscape. Their water channels change by the hour as powerful tides advance and retreat. Complex deltas form and re-form, a balance between the forces of river and sea.

When a fast-flowing river carrying a vast load of mud and silt enters the sea – or even a lake – it drops its cargo. The biggest stones are dropped first, followed by finer material, most of which falls to the

HOW A GEYSER WORKS

NATURE'S HOT WATER SPOUTS

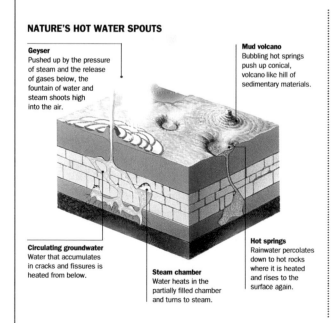

Geyser
Pushed up by the pressure of steam and the release of gases below, the fountain of water and steam shoots high into the air.

Mud volcano
Bubbling hot springs push up conical, volcano like hill of sedimentary materials.

Circulating groundwater
Water that accumulates in cracks and fissures is heated from below.

Steam chamber
Water heats in the partially filled chamber and turns to steam.

Hot springs
Rainwater percolates down to hot rocks where it is heated and rises to the surface again.

Geysers are powerful spouts of boiling water that shoot up from the ground at regular intervals in volcanic regions, or in regions where volcanoes have been active in the recent past. Groundwater (rain that has soaked into the ground) trickles down towards a magma chamber – a body of cooling molten rock deep underground. The water is heated beyond boiling point, and the steam forces it back up to the surface with immense force. Old Faithful in Yellowstone Park, USA, gushes forth every 65 minutes – the time it takes for the steam pressure to build up in its underground reservoir.

POOLS OF STEAM *Steaming water has formed the 'Minerva Terraces' at Yellowstone's Mammoth Hot Springs.*

sea bed in the deeper water a little farther out. Deltas form whenever rivers drop sediments faster than the sea can remove them. Not all of the sediment, however, will be deposited in the sea: the river will drop some in its own bed, particularly during storms and periods of low water, forcing it to cut new channels for itself. As the old channels dry out and vegetation takes root, new land is formed and the coastline slowly pushes out into the sea.

Deltas can develop in lakes, ponds and even small pools on the seashore, where the whole process may take place in an afternoon, but the big river deltas have been forming for millions of years. The delta of the Ganges and Brahmaputra rivers has filled in a large part of the Bay of Bengal. The Indus has gradually formed most of Pakistan from the eroded material of the Himalayas, which it has carried and dumped into the Arabian Sea. The Nile has carried detritus from Ethiopia for thousands of miles and built the Nile delta out into the Mediterranean Sea.

In North America, the Mississippi has formed the continent's central lowlands by continuously building its deltas out into the Gulf of Mexico. But it does not matter whether the delta is as big as the Mississippi or as small as a beach pool: the building process is similar.

Throughout history, deltas have been a focus for people. Those of the Tigris–Euphrates, the Nile and the Indus were the sites of early civilisations. They provided people with fertile soils on which to grow their crops. Today dam-building, irrigation projects and deforestation are upsetting natural cycle and deltas are being destroyed. The Nile delta has retreated, for example, after the building of the Aswan Dam. The sediment, scooped up and transported along the 4160 miles (6695 km) of the river, does not reach the sea but is now trapped in the artificial lake behind the dam. In the delta, area erosion by the sea is winning the battle and the delta is slowly disappearing.

In Bangladesh, people have lived on the largest delta in the world for thousands of years and have been dependent for their survival on the crops grown on the rich soils deposited by the Ganges and Brahmaputra rivers.

In recent times, flood waters have frequently rushed down from deforested slopes inland and overwhelmed the coastal strip. The floods, combined with the sea's encroachment on these low-lying lands and the effects of monsoon storms, make the delta – one of the most highly populated places on Earth – one of the most vulnerable as well.

Bangladesh, where the delta makes up most of the country, has indeed suffered more than its share of disasters. In 1970, a combination of cyclone and flood waters cost 200 000 people their lives. In 1974, floods submerged an area of Bangladesh the size of Texas and Louisiana combined.

DUMPING THE MUD *Low tide reveals vast river-delta mud flats at King Sound in Western Australia.*

MOVING SANDS

owering over the desert like ocean waves frozen in time are great mounds of shifting sand known as 'dunes'. Forests, farms, and even sometimes entire towns are smothered by these constantly moving mountains, which account in total for about 5 million sq miles (13 million km²) of the Earth's surface, an area twice the size of the USA.

The dunes are blown by the winds, sometimes in violent sandstorms that scrape the paint from cars and slice through telephone lines. The sands move fast and far, depending on the strength and direction of the wind. Of the two main types, crescent-shaped dunes or 'barchans' form when the wind blows only in one direction, while 'seif' dunes resemble the surface of a rough sea. Some dunes are shaped like elongated mounds, running in parallel lines and separated by rocky corridors; they may stretch for 100 miles (160 km) or more.

The shallow troughs of the Sahara, known as 'ergs', have some of the largest of all dunes. Winds from many directions deposit their sand in great star-shaped heaps, sometimes more than 1000 ft (305 m) high. These huge peaks stay put for many years, serving as landmarks for desert travellers.

Most dunes, however, are constantly on the move. A dune creeps forward as sand blown up the gently sloping upwind side spills over the crest and builds up at the top of the unstable steep slope. When this slope reaches an angle of about 34°, the sand cascades down its face. With crescent-shaped dunes, sand on the flanks moves faster than that in the centre, the sickle shape emphasised by higher wind speeds along the outer edges of the dune. As long as the wind is blowing, the process continues over and over again, to the extent that dunes can climb a slope of 25° to form a ramp leading up to a high plateau. The sand grains themselves are rounded and move easily in the wind.

Even deserts have 'seasons', since the formation and movement of sand dunes is dependent on seasonal wind patterns. In the Wahibah Desert of Oman scientists on a British Royal Geographical Society expedition found that sand movement is greatest in the summer when the south-west monsoon winds blow the sand towards the north-east at a rate of about 10 ft (3 m) in ten days. And when the sand moves, it does not go piecemeal: instead, entire dunes retain their valleys and ridges and move in one great mass. In winter and spring, when the winds blow from different directions, the dune crests form and

re-form, moving along at a rate of about 3 ft (1 m) each day.

In some places, sand is stopped in its tracks by a natural obstruction. Witsand, in the Kalahari Desert of southern Africa, is an island of white sand dunes, 6 miles (10 km) long and 2 miles (3 km) wide, in a sea of red sand. A row of quartzite *kopjes* – outcrops of rock in an otherwise featureless landscape – have trapped the sands blowing from the Kalahari and a range of low sand

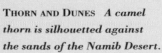
THORN AND DUNES *A camel thorn is silhouetted against the sands of the Namib Desert.*

mountains have gradually accumulated. Water, trapped in the quartzite and seeping up from it, bleaches the sand white or a grey-blue colour that contrasts strongly with the oxide-rich sands of the surrounding desert. Local superstition has it that the white sand will not mix with the red. The magic is enhanced by the presence of curious stalacmite-like formations. They occur where lightning has struck the sand, fusing the sand particles together into misshapen tubes known as fulgurites.

Sand dunes are not always the products of hot deserts. Coastal dunes made from rocky fragments ground into a fine sand by the action of the sea may be pushed back from the coast by onshore gales. The legacy of glaciers includes wind-blown fragments of shattered rock sculpted by cold winds after the Ice Age into huge dune fields like those along Lake Michigan in North America and in parts of Germany and the Netherlands. A storm in 1775 buried the church of Skagen on the northernmost tip of Jutland in Denmark in sand, leaving only its tower poking through. In the hotter parts of southern Europe, dunes up to 100 ft (30 m) high are sometimes swept up into the sky, burying green forests and ancient buildings alike.

SHELTER IN THE SAHARA *Oases vary from a few palm trees round a well to hundreds of square miles of fertile land.*

Dunes also make mysterious sounds. The sands squeak, rumble and roar. The sounds are created when accumulated heaps of sunbaked sand break up and tumble down the steep face of a dune. When sand grains are analysed under powerful electron microscopes, scientists have discovered that those from 'booming' dunes or 'singing' sands are more polished than those from other dunes.

LINES IN THE SAND *Sand and light create striking patterns in the dunes of Algeria's Grand Erg.*

GIANT SCULPTURES

Earth pillars and limestone pinnacles, rock arches and rock towers, giant boulders and moorland tors – all are strewn carelessly about the Earth's landscapes, the legacy of many centuries of erosion by wind, water and ice.

The elements water, ice and wind shape the planet's rocks into forms as spectacular and breathtaking as anything achieved by a human sculptor. In areas where erosion is fast, or where there is little vegetation cover, protrusions of bare rock frequently pierce the landscape. As often as not, these weird-looking objects have become part of folklore – the Devil is a favourite culprit when seeking to explain the seemingly unexplainable. Clusters of rock are sometimes said to be young women who have fallen from the path of virtue, or defeated armies turned into stone for their sins and cowardice. Others, such as the Old Man of Hoy in the islands of Orkney off north-eastern Scotland, are more benign figures, seen as guardians of the landscape.

Ice is a ferocious weathering agent of rock, and not just in polar regions. Water,

seeping into any open pore or fissure in a rock will expand as it freezes, pushing outwards at the rock as it does so. After several periods of freeze-and-thaw, fragments of the rock fall off.

In desert regions, where freezing temperatures are not uncommon at night, dew or water from occasional rainstorms will disintegrate rocks as efficiently as any sledgehammer. As a result, sizable screes (loose rock debris) accumulate at the foot of cliffs, and vast tracts of desert consist of bare rock littered with stones. In fact, deserts are shaped to a surprising degree by water. Rainfall is a rarity in a desert, but when it arrives it falls in torrents. With little or no vegetation to hold it in place, loose material is swept away by the water.

From a flash flood in the desert to the gentle flow of a river, flowing water sweeps along pebbles, stones or grains of sand, all of which collide with other rocks, and contribute to the shaping effect of water on the landscape. As well as dissolving rock, water also creates cavities and disintegration. This effect is more marked if it contains dissolved carbon dioxide from the air – which attacks limestone – or organic acids from the soil, which attack the mineral feldspar, a major constituent of granite. Chemical weathering such as this usually produces rounded lines.

The wind, too, can transport a powerful load of abrasive sand, carrying most of it along a yard or less above the ground. Consequently, the sandblasting effect is most pronounced at lower levels, sometimes leaving large blocks of rock perched precariously on a narrow base. Wind-blown sand accentuates any variations in rock hardness – as do water and ice. Softer rock is stripped away, leaving harder strata exposed behind. Flat-bedded sedimentary rocks end up in totem-pole shapes, or as odd stumps. Igneous rocks (such as granite or basalt, formed when molten rock solidifies) may end up as razor-sharp monoliths.

Leaving the eroded areas scoured and bare, wind, ice and water transport the fragments of rock, sand and dust and deposit them far away as fresh sediment that will one day become rock.

THE SILENT MULTITUDE OF BRYCE CANYON

PINNACLES OF LIMESTONE ROCK

STAND UP IN STRANGE SHAPES

'Red rocks standing up like men in a bowl-shaped canyon' – for centuries, that was the name the local Paiute Indians used for a vast rock amphitheatre standing on the eastern edge of the Paunsaugunt Plateau in southern Utah. To the Paiute, the rocks were men who had been punished by the

THE PINNACLES *Limestone pillars dot Western Australia's Nam Bung Park.*

FIGURES ON THE HILLSIDE
Gnarled and crumbling pinnacles huddle on the slopes of Utah's Bryce Canyon.

gods and turned to stone. Bryce Canyon – as the place is now named, after an early European settler in the region – conjures up surreal images: an ancient city of minarets . . . a group of cathedral spires . . . a silent multitude of hooded figures.

Sixty million years ago, Bryce Canyon lay on the bed of a shallow freshwater lake. For 15 million years, sand, shell and silt settled on the bottom until there was a layer of rock composed of limestone, mudstone and shale almost 1000 ft (300 m) thick. Finally, subterranean movements thrust the rock upwards to about 9000 ft (2750 m) above sea level, forming the high tablelands and plateaus we see today. Despite the violent movement, the beds of rock stayed almost horizontal.

Ever since, erosion has been shaping the canyon. Melting snow and rainwater washed away the softer mudstone and shale and carved steep-sided channels, some of which are 500 ft (150 m) deep. The edge of the plateau is cut into a series of pinnacles and knife-shaped ridges, exposing the many different layers of rock – each a different colour. The red rocks have the most iron; the purplish ones have manganese.

SETTING FOR ADVENTURE *Cracked and timeworn sandstone resulted in Venezuela's* tepuí *peaks.*

At sunrise and sunset, Bryce Canyon is transformed: the low angle of the Sun lends an astonishing richness to the colours, which are enhanced by the shadows of the fantastic rock shapes.

'ISLAND' MOUNTAINS IN A RAINFOREST

FLAT-TOPPED PEAKS AND A MIGHTY WATERFALL: A SETTING FOR ADVENTURE

In 1912, Sir Arthur Conan Doyle wrote *The Lost World*, a science-fiction adventure story set in a land of flat-topped, sheer-sided mountains rising thousands of feet above the forest floor. The inspiration for this setting came from around Mount Roraima, a flat-topped peak 9097 ft (2772 m) above sea level, at the point where the borders of eastern Venezuela, Brazil and Guyana meet. Stretching north and west are the tropical forests of La Gran Sabana, whose rivers are tributaries of the Orinoco.

Warm, wet winds from the Atlantic are forced to rise above these peaks, which causes a high rainfall on the mountain-tops – about 300 in (7620 mm) a year. This feeds the streams crashing down from the heights, the most famous of which is from Auyán-Tepuí (Devil's Mountain), 9842 ft (2950 m) above sea level. The water falls in two cascades: a clear drop, first, of 2650 ft (807 m), followed by a second one of more than 560 ft (170 m). Together, they are nearly 18 times higher than Niagara and constitute the world's highest waterfall.

These falls from Devil's Mountain are called the Angel Falls after an American ex-World War I pilot, Jimmie Angel, who was first shown them by a local gold prospector. On a later trip in 1935, he landed his small aircraft on top of the mountain and was unable to take off again. After some weeks he and his two companions struggled back to their camp, leaving the plane rotting in the sodden vegetation on top of Auyán-Tepuí. It was later brought down, and can now been seen in a local museum.

The region's tabletopped mountains are known as *tepuís* – the name given to them by the local Pemón people. They are made from sandstone, formed from debris eroded from ancient mountains 2 billion years ago. The debris was compressed into rock and formed a bed of sandstone that was pushed up by major earth movements. Cracks and fissures within the rock have been attacked over millions of years by wind and rain, and the weaker sections have been worn away. Now only 100 or so sheer-sided, sandstone blocks survive, towering above the surrounding forest like islands in a sea of green.

Like islands, *tepuís* have been isolated for millions of years, their plants and animals quite distinct from those in the forest below. In fact, each *tepuí* has its own animals and plants, about half the species of which are unique. Caves, crumbling cliffs, bogs and fast-flowing rivers and streams make the *tepuís* inaccessible, and even an approach by helicopter is fraught with danger due to dangerous air currents, dense fogs and sudden rainstorms. And so we can expect many more discoveries to be made in these 'Lost Worlds'.

GRANITE PEAKS IN THE ANDES

CHILE'S PAINE TOWERS LOOM AT THE EDGES OF THE ANDES

At the southern end of the Andes, near the borders of Chile and Argentina, loom the Paine Towers. The three colossal peaks stand in relative isolation, the central and highest one rising to 8758 ft (2670 m) above sea level. Often wreathed in cloud

GRANITE PEAKS *Movements in the depths of the Earth forced up the peaks of the Andes' Paine Massif.*

and battered by storms, they form part of the Paine Massif – a cluster of jagged mountains carved by glaciers. Nearby is another group: the Paine Horns, granite mountains tipped in places with black slate.

About 200 million years ago the granite was a molten mass surrounded by slate deep in the Earth's crust. The granite solidified, and since then the slate has eroded, revealing the reddish-brown granite peaks of today.

The Andes were formed by the collision of the South American and Pacific plates of the Earth's crust – and the Paine Towers are part of that movement. As the Pacific plate dives beneath the South American plate, it ruckles up the edge of the continent to form the Andean chain, which rises to nearly 23 000 ft (7000 m). Offshore, the sinking crust drags the ocean floor down to depths of over 26 240 ft (8000 m). Glaciers are still carving the dramatic outline of the massif.

The Paine Towers lie in the wind belt known as the 'Furious Fifties' (lying between latitudes 50° and 60° South), where westerly winds are even stormier than in the 'Roaring Forties' (lying between 40° and 50° South). Their remote situation and the fierce weather conditions meant that for a long time few people had ever seen the Towers, let alone climbed them – probably a more difficult conquest than Everest. In 1958, however, an Italian team led by Guido Monzino scaled the north Tower, and five years later, Chris Bonington and Don Whillans led a British expedition that climbed the central peak.

The name 'Paine' – it is pronounced 'pie-nay' – is something of a mystery. Some say it comes from the word for 'pink' in the language of an extinct local tribe,

HOW A TOR IS FORMED

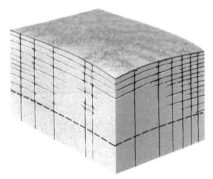

A block of solid granite is exposed to the elements.

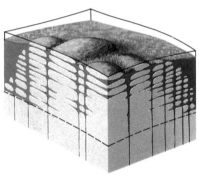

Feldspar, a mineral embedded in the granite, disintegrates into china clay.

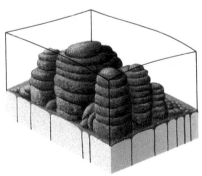

The china clay is washed away by water and wind erosion, leaving a tor.

Tors develop when surrounding softer rocks erode, exposing a granite core, formed by the cooling of molten rock. The white mineral feldspar, embedded in cracks and crevices within the granite, disintegrates in its turn, to form china clay or Kaolin – used in medicine, paper- and textile-making, and ceramics. It is washed away, leaving behind large untouched blocks of granite: the tors.

BALANCING ACT *Piles of granite take unexpected shapes on Dartmoor in the west of England.*

referring to the pinkish tints of the granite. Others believe it was the name of an early European settler in the region.

WHEN NATURE APPEARS TO DEFY GRAVITY

GRANITE TORS MARK THE SITE OF LONG-LOST MOUNTAINS

Around 300 million years ago, France and southern Britain were involved in the same type of continental collision that is still forming the Himalayas. The mountains

that resulted may have been just as high as the Himalayas, but the temperatures deep inside were so high that the rocks melted. The melt cooled slowly to form a rock composed of large, interlocking crystals – a grey and white granite.

Since then, time and weathering have stripped mountains down to their granite cores on the moors of Cornwall and Devon: Land's End, Carnmenellis, St Austell, Bodmin and Dartmoor. Each of these moors is capped by tors – massive boulders piled up as if by some legendary giant.

STRANGE SENTINELS IN MONO LAKE

PINNACLES OF TUFA ARE REVEALED BY THE LOWERING WATER LEVEL

In 1863, the writer Mark Twain, who was also once a steamboat pilot, nearly lost his life in Mono Lake – 'this solemn, silent,

MONO STATUARY *'Tufa' pinnacles rise from California's Mono Lake.*

sailless sea – this lonely tenant of the loneliest spot on Earth'.

Mono Lake lies east of San Francisco on the eastern slopes of the Sierra Nevada. It fills a basin formed 700 000 years ago by the folding of the mountains and volcanic activity. It has hot springs and jets of steam, and as the hot, mineral-rich water meets the lake's cooler water, the chemicals are precipitated out as a rock called 'tufa', which forms pillars and pinnacles. Since Mono Lake has no outlet, the natural salts washed into it are added to the existing volcanic chemicals to make a concentrated brine too salty even for fish.

The lake's ecosystem is now protected.

Many streams in the Sierra Nevada have been dammed to deliver water to the coastal cities, including streams supplying Mono Lake. In the past 50 years, the water level has fallen by about 40 ft (12 m). Now there are dusty salt flats lining the shores.

BALANCING BOULDERS IN NORTHERN ITALY

RITTEN EARTH PILLARS – A QUIRK OF THE ICE AGE AND MEDIEVAL KNIGHTS

Large boulders perch precariously on tall pinnacles of rock in an Alpine valley of northern Italy. They look strangely like the soaring spires of several Gothic cathedrals.

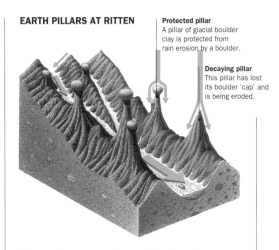

EARTH PILLARS AT RITTEN

Protected pillar
A pillar of glacial boulder clay is protected from rain erosion by a boulder.

Decaying pillar
This pillar has lost its boulder 'cap' and is being eroded.

ALPINE ABSTRACTS *Caps of hard gneiss rock protect the clay beneath them.*

About 30 million years ago, an ocean lying between Africa and northern Europe closed, thrusting up the Alps. Then, 2 million years ago, came the Ice Age. Glaciers wound their way from the mountaintops scouring the rocks as they went. When the ice melted, it dumped a mixture of clay and rock.

Since then, fast-flowing rivers have eroded deep gulleys in this 'boulder clay'. The clay is soft and washes away easily, but the boulders, made of gneiss – a hard, coarse-grained rock – are left behind. Perched on top of the rock, they act like umbrellas, protecting the clay beneath, which stands up as pillars.

FLYING BUTTRESS *Strange formations abound in Utah's Arches National Park.*

A WAVE SCULPTED IN AUSTRALIAN ROCK

Some people call it the 'surfers' dream wave'. But Wave Rock in Western Australia lies about 186 miles (300 km) from the sea, and is in fact a ridge of yellowish granite about 120 ft (37 m) long and 50 ft (15 m) high. The curving face of the 'wave' was shaped by wind and water: the wind blasted sand grains against it; rainwater trickled over and through the rock after storms. As the water soaked through the granite, it dissolved some of the chemicals in it and redeposited them on the surface, staining the rock with long curving lines of reddish brown. Standing nearby, and dwarfed by the overhanging curl of the granite, it is easy to imagine that the wave is just about to break.

POWER OF THE ELEMENTS *Wind and water shaped Wave Rock in Western Australia.*

Why, then, are these strange pillars not found elsewhere in the Alps? The answer seems to lie with people. German knights who settled in Ritten in the 13th century cleared trees to farm the slopes. But the trees and their roots had provided an extra protective cover for clay and boulders alike that survived in other valleys.

STONE ARCHES SCULPTED BY WATER

ARCHES IN UTAH'S DESERT – WHERE NATURE'S WORK LOOKS LIKE MAN'S

Just west of the Colorado River, in the state of Utah, the rust-coloured desert reveals a group of naturally formed arches. The Arches National Park has over 2000 of them, with names ranging from the Delicate Arch and the Eye of the Whale to the Windows Arch and Landscape Arch.

Around 150 million years ago, there was a salty inland lake here. It lay in a bed of sand, cemented by calcium carbonate and iron salts. Under this layer of sandstone was another of salt. When the lake dried, some of the chemicals cementing the sandstone were dissolved. The harsh climate began to do the rest.

In winter the saturated rock freezes, the ice crystals expand, and the rock flakes and crumbles. In the heat of summer, salt in the rock turns to crystal that expands and pushes upwards. Over millions of years, the combined effect has carved the red rock into the mysterious shapes of today's landscape.

Nature in Colour 2

ROCK PATTERNS *Ribbed bands stripe the rock in the Antelope Canyon in Arizona.*

VIEWED FROM SATELLITES IN SPACE, TWO-THIRDS OF THE EARTH'S SURFACE IS THE COLOUR OF THE BLUE SEA. MUCH OF THE REST OF THE PLANET IS A MIXTURE OF DUSTY BROWNS FROM ITS DESERTS AND WHITE FROM ICE AND SNOW. TUNDRA BLOTCHES LARGE AREAS, WHILE THE REMAINDER OF EARTH'S SURFACE IS FILLED WITH THE GREENS OF TREES AND GRASS. VIEWED MORE CLOSELY, EARTH'S ROCKS REVEAL A FURTHER SYMPHONY OF COLOUR: IRON REDS, SULPHUR YELLOWS AND COPPER BLUES. FROM EARTH LOOKING UPWARDS, MEANWHILE, IS THE ARID DARKNESS OF SPACE, BUT IT, TOO, CAN PROVIDE SPECTACULAR NATURAL DISPLAYS OF LIGHT AND COLOUR, SUCH AS SHOOTING STARS AND THE NORTHERN AND SOUTHERN LIGHTS.

HIGH LIGHT *Reflected sunlight glows in a 'night shining' cloud.*

COLOURS OF THE EARTH

Seen from space, the Earth is the 'blue planet'. But on its surface it is much more richly hued, with black and white sands, red and green sandstones, multicoloured minerals, and rocks that seem to change colour according to the light.

A careful look at any landscape reveals a kaleidoscope of colour – the colours of soils, plants, water, sky, all picked out in subtly differing hues as the light changes over the course of the day. The colours are produced in many ways. Those of rocks and soils tend to be dominated by the minerals they contain: iron stains red and brown; copper tints rocks green; sulphur makes them yellow. When the Sun is low on the horizon at dawn and dusk, and its light passes through more of the atmosphere, dust particles scatter the light and make reds and oranges appear more intense. At midday, full sunlight can turn a red rock amber.

Desert rocks are coated with blackish or brownish stains coming from iron and manganese oxides known as 'desert varnish'. The coating is also found on the rocks in waterfalls along great rivers such as the Nile in Africa and the Orinoco in South America, suggesting that these deserts were once much wetter than they are now.

Rocks are also coloured by living organisms, such as algae and lichens that live on the surface and in cracks. In the Antarctic, organisms live inside the rock. Sandstones in the so-called 'dry valleys' of Victoria Land, south of New Zealand, have black streaks of lichen, white layers of fungus and green veins of blue-green algae living in pores inside the rock. Even Antarctic snow need not be white. In the southern spring, the snow can be coloured pink by snow algae.

SANDSTONE DRAMA *Swirling lines are carved in red stone in Colorado.*

Similarly, oceans, seas, lakes and ponds are coloured by the sediments that pour into them from rivers and streams. Other colouring agents are the 'blooms' of plant plankton, such as red dinoflagellates (red algae) and green algae.

SOLITARY SPLENDOUR AT AYERS ROCK

BATHED IN SUNLIGHT, IT GLOWS WITH EVER-CHANGING COLOURS

One of the Southern Hemisphere's most spectacular sights is Ayers Rock, the largest sandstone monolith in the world rising from the desert of Australia's Northern Territory. As the sunlight plays across it, the rock undergoes radiant transitions from bright orange to a darkening crimson. At its richest, it appears to be incandescent, as if lit from inside by molten lava. Ayers Rock is a sacred site to the country's Aboriginal people, who call it Uluru. It was officially restored to them in 1985.

At places such as Ayers Rock, the different colours of the rock are the result of the Sun shining on different stones within it – stones that are as variable as marble and granite. Marble alone can range in colour from the purest white to the deepest black, passing through a spectrum of pinks, yellows, greens, blues, violets and reds on the way.

The colour of a stone is determined as much by its physical nature as its chemical composition, since it is the geometrical

THE ROCK THAT CHANGES COLOUR *Ayers Rock (Uluru) in Australia's Northern Territory can be dull grey at dawn, sandy brown under the noonday sun and a shining red at sunset. Rising 1142 ft (348 m) above the surrounding plain and measuring 5 miles (8 km) around its base, it is all that now remains of a sandstone mountain which has been worn down over the millennia by wind-blown sand. Its changing colours are the result of sunlight reflecting off different stones embedded in it at different times of the day.*

LAYER-CAKE MOUNTAINS
Racoon-striped slopes rise from the Painted Desert of Arizona. Different coloured shales, marls and sandstones create the desert's kaleidoscope landscape.

structure that controls how the rock absorbs or reflects particular wave-lengths of light. Any variation in its structure, no matter how small, will often yield different colours. As the quality of the light changes with the approach of dawn or dusk, so the colour of rock also seems to change. One result of this is that the geologist can never rely on colour as a foolproof means of identifying a rock.

The Earth, with its single sun and relatively few minerals, would be a monotonous place if sunlight was constant. Fortunately, climate, season and location, as well as different types of rocks and their response to light, are all part of the paintbox that combines with the Sun to create nature's colourful canvases.

Despite its name, Ayers Rock is not one gigantic stone, but an inselberg – literally, an 'island mountain' – that has been shaped by wind-blown sands. It is all that remains of sandstone mountains that were pushed up 500 million years ago. The surface is not smooth, but covered with parallel grooves, pockmarked

WHAT CAUSES ROCK COLOUR?

Iron gives much of the landscape its colour, since iron is the commonest 'dye' in most rocks. The colour it stains them varies, however, according to how much oxygen it is mixed with. The rock-forming iron-based mineral haematite, for example, with comparatively low levels of oxygen, is a rich brownish-red colour; limonite, with more oxygen in it, is a yellow ochre colour.

Mixed in varying proportions, these two minerals can give a landscape an astonishing range of colour, from the deep red of the Aswan granite forming the Nile's first cataract, to the warm creams and honey colours of the limestones that form most of the gently rolling hills of northern Europe.

Without oxygen, iron gives either a black or greenish tinge. Volcanic ash containing iron that has come to rest in water often takes on a vivid shade of sage green. Other striking colours occur when less common minerals are present. Copper shades rock green or blue; manganese and cobalt are pink; chromium and cadmium are orange; and mercury colours red.

The colours of the minerals themselves are determined by the behaviour of light. Light reflects off the surface of a stable metal such as gold, revealing its basic yellow colour. An unstable metal such as silver, by contrast, often has a coating of a different colour.

The colour of a transparent crystal, meanwhile, is created in two ways. First, light and other forms of radiation interact with atomic particles such as electrons to give the mineral its colour. The greenish hue of the gemstone peridot – traditionally regarded as the birth-stone for August – is created like this. Alternatively, the mineral obtains its colour when tainted with impurities, such as the reddish colours in orthoclase, a crystalline mineral often found in granite.

Microscopic particles in minerals may also cause the light to scatter in interesting ways, as in a moonstone or in the star reflections in rubies and sapphires. Thus diamonds have 'fire' – rapidly changing flashes of colour that are the result of white light being broken up into its component colours as it passes through the crystal. Diamonds are cut in such a way as to accentuate the effect.

LIGHT ON ROCK *Polarised light is reflected through a slice of schist rock.*

with caves and fissures, and streaked with black runnels where water runs away after infrequent rainstorms.

ARIZONA'S PAINTED DESERT

THE SHIFTING COLOURS OF DESERT SANDSTONE ARE FIRED BY LIGHT

Red rocks 'glow' most intensely at sunset; green and blue rocks are seen to best advantage at dawn. Noonday fades out colour contrasts, while the Moon enhances light colours. Every rock has its ideal light. But, by the same token, some scenery can have no ideal light, thanks to its very variety.

The multicoloured sandstone landscapes of the Painted Desert of Arizona are a case in point. Here, every change in the colour of sandstone is the result of some subtle alteration in the climate, with

LAGOON COLOURS IN THE ANDES
Bolivia's Laguna Colorado
spreads out white and tomato red.

centuries of erosion and sedimentation forever revealing different layers of stone.

Sometimes the desert air glows pink or purple with dusts derived from brightly coloured shales, marls and sandstones. The desert is banded with vividly coloured rock strata shaded red, yellow, blue, white and lavender, and the Navaho and Hopi Indians, who have reservations there, use the multicoloured sands for ceremonial sand paintings.

THE COLOURED LAGOON IN SOUTH AMERICA

A TOMATO-RED 'SOUP' OF MICROSCOPIC ALGAE FILLS A BOWL IN THE ANDES

The Laguna Colorado, or 'coloured lagoon', in the Bolivian Andes looks like a vast bowl of tomato soup, with remnants of cream around the rim.

The tomato red of the 'soup' is due to a rich concentration of microscopic plants and animals in the water; the 'cream' is a

sludge of salt and gypsum. Other deposits are derived from the streams and rivers that enter the lake after eroding and dissolving rocks in the nearby mountains. For much of the time the colour is non-existent, as the lake evaporates to become a dazzling basin of salt.

The same phenomenon, but less spectacular, gave the Red Sea its name. In other red lagoons, particularly in Lake Natron in the Great Rift Valley of East Africa, the algae provides a rich source of food for flamingos. Their specially adapted beaks enable them to filter the vegetable matter from the sludge. The presence of beta-carotenoids in the algae also gives the birds their pink plumage, adding colour to their strutting elegance.

On the Indonesian island of Flores, three lakes nestling in the craters of the extinct volcano Keli Mutu change colour and nobody knows why. Today one is black, another dark green and the third light green, but in the 1960s one was coffee-

coloured, the second red-brown, and the other blue. The local people believe the souls respectively of magicians, of criminals and of virgins and infants live in the lakes.

WHITE SANDS OF NEW MEXICO

WIND-BLOWN GYPSUM SHIMMERS LIKE A DESERT OF SNOW

Most sand dunes are formed from tiny, wind-blown particles of the hard, crystalline mineral quartz. But on the broad, flat floor of the Tularosa Valley in New Mexico, they are made from gypsum, a mineral that is almost pure white in colour.

Elsewhere in the world, deposits of gypsum have been mined, removed and used by the building trade in plaster, plaster of Paris and plasterboard. But White Sands, New Mexico (whose other claim to fame is that the first atomic bomb was exploded just 40 miles – 64 km – to its north in July 1945), is remote and for a long time remained nearly inaccessible; it thus escaped exploitation. Since 1933, this vast 275 sq mile (712 km²) gypsum desert has been a US national monument, and it is now a protected area.

The gypsum was washed from the rocks

SAND THAT LOOKS LIKE SNOW *These desertspoons are poking out from white gypsum sand in New Mexico.*

of the nearby San Andres Mountains and accumulated on the bed of the now waterless Lake Lucero. Evaporation, aided by sun and wind, caused the lake to dry up, and the coarse fragments of gypsum were ground into finer particles as they were blown about by the swirling winds. Vast quantities of gypsum sand lie in the valley and it has been pushed up into dunes over 100 ft (30m) high. Blown by the prevailing winds, they are moving steadily to the north-east at a rate of some 20 ft (6m) each year.

Some of the creatures living in the desert have adapted to their background of white. The bleached earless lizard and the Apache pocket mouse are both coloured white. Their camouflage helps protect them from the attention of passing hawks and eagles.

BLACK TROPICAL SANDS

VOLCANIC ASH FORMS AN UNUSUAL PARADISE BEACH

Most holiday brochures draw attention to a resort's 'miles of golden sands', but beaches can be almost any colour, depending on the underlying bedrock. Some, indeed, are pure black or white. In temperate climates, beaches tend to be the traditional golden

A BEACH OF ANY OTHER HUE . . . *Waves crash onto black volcanic sands on Lanzarote in the Canary Islands.*

colour, consisting of ground-down crystalline quartz containing various iron oxide 'impurities'. Shell beaches, coral beaches and those at the edge of warm shallow seas, by contrast, are composed mainly of the skeletons of dead marine organisms and, being made of calcium carbonate, appear pure white.

On volcanic islands the sand is sometimes black, betraying its origin as volcanic ash or the ground-up debris from dark-coloured basaltic rocks and lava. The Canary Islands, for example, are cones that were formed by extinct volcanoes. There are comparatively few beaches on these rocky outposts in the ocean, but among them some have black sand. Similarly, surf and wind action have

reduced the dark basaltic lavas of Hawaii to black sands, as at Kalapana, on Hawaii island's south-east coast.

SALT DEPOSITS IN ETHIOPIA

FROM TIME TO TIME A MULTICOLOURED LAKE FORMS IN A HOT SALT DESERT

The Danakil Depression, in the north-east corner of Ethiopia, was once part of the nearby Red Sea. But major movements of the Earth's surface pushed up the nearby Danakil Highlands, and the depression was cut off to form Lake Karum, a salt-water lake about 45 miles (72 km) wide. The water in the lake evaporated, leaving a layer of salt over 2 miles (3 km) thick in places. For most of the time the blinding

WATERS OF FIRE *Hot volcanic springs create striking patterns on Lake Karum in north-east Ethiopia.*

white salt surface is dry, but rainwater does occasionally wash down from the plateau to the west, forming a brine-rich lake, 400 ft (120 m) below sea level.

The rain also percolates down to pockets of molten magma below the Earth's surface, and the superheated water re-erupts at the surface as searing hot springs that stain the rocks red, brown or yellow according to the minerals contained in them. The local people – the Afars – mine the salt, which is transported by camel train to Makale and thence to towns and villages all over Africa.

Changing Colours of the Sea

The Black Sea is not black and the White Sea is not white, but the Red Sea is sometimes red. Occasionally, tiny red marine organisms, known as dinoflagellates, reproduce in such numbers that they colour the entire sea red.

A red tide occurs when there is a super-abundance of nutrients in the water and continuous sunshine. When this happens, there can be well over 300 million individual dinoflagellates for every gallon of sea water (70 million per litre), turning the sea a red or brown colour. But when a bloom reaches these proportions it becomes dangerous to people and animals. A large bloom not only uses up most of the oxygen in the water, causing fish to become asphyxiated, but each tiny dinoflagellate produces virulent poisons. In 1946, a red tide off Florida caused the death of an estimated 50 million fish, and many people suffered food poisoning from eating contaminated mussels and clams.

Red tides aside, the oceans mainly appear blue. Clear, blue waters, however, contain few nutrients to sustain life, whereas the surface layers of murky green seas are packed with green chlorophyll-containing phytoplankton that turn sunlight, water and carbon dioxide into sugars – this makes them the foundation of numerous marine food chains. Most life in the sea, and maybe much of life on Earth,

BLUE AND SHINING *Deep blue marks out the underwater cavern of a 'blue hole' off Belize (above). Tiny glowing organisms create ocean phosphorescence (below).*

American scholar and statesman Benjamin Franklin concluded that it was an electrical discharge between water and salt.

Sometimes, phosphorescence at the sea's surface is in the form of a gigantic wheel, up to a mile (1.6 km) or more in diameter, with waves of luminescence moving outwards like the ripples in a pool. The wheels may start with an explosion of flashing lights and spread outwards, rotating like the wheel of a bicycle. These phenomena may be the result of disturbances by small-scale undersea earthquakes on the seafloor.

Not all seas are coloured by living things. Rain leaches minerals from rocks, and rivers wash debris down to the sea. The Yellow Sea is aptly named, for sediments washed down by rivers from the Chinese mainland stain its waters a dirty yellow.

One of the most extraordinary of sea colours is found in the mystery 'muds' or 'whitings' of the Great Bahama Bank. Whitings are huge patches of milky water found in the sea to the west of Andros and Abaco islands. They resemble clouds in a blue sky, appearing to the crews of yachts as shallow white sandbanks in waters up to 30 ft (9 m) deep. What causes them is hotly debated by rival scientists.

The local belief is that they are caused by enormous shoals of small fish – 'whitings' – that disturb the bottom deposits. The sediments are formed from the dead bodies of millions of minute algae, known as *Penicillus*, that form crystals of chalk inside their tiny bodies. When they die the cells rot and the needle-shaped crystals fall to the seabed. The fish stir them up – or so one of the theories suggests. But the only fish to be seen regularly in the whitings are sharks, not ordinary grey or grey-blue ones but snow-white sharks about 3 ft (1 m) long. They swim through the white patches of sea invisible except for the black tips to their dorsal fins. Exactly what lies behind the whitings and their strangely adapted pure white sharks remains a mystery.

BLUE-GREEN TIDE *The 25 000-odd species of algae make colourful ocean dyes.*

depends on their well-being. In temperate regions, the sea appears blue in winter but often turns green in spring when new life proliferates in it.

At night the sea's surface can glow with an eerie green, purple or yellow light. This is because of countless tiny luminescent organisms that flash when disturbed, as in the wake of a whale swimming at the surface. It leaves a long trail of intense green 'phosphorescence' from dinoflagellates and comb jellies bursting into light like underwater fireworks. The ghostly glow has sparked off many a tale: the Romans considered it an evil omen; the Bretons believed that the phosphorescence came from the glitter of precious stones in an undersea garden where the sea-god placed the souls of drowned men. Even science was baffled for a long time. In the 7th century AD it was thought that the glow was the result of the sea absorbing sunlight by day and emitting it at night. The

WHITE ON WHITE *Milky white seas on the Grand Bahama Bank (right) are home to specially adapted, 3 ft (1 m) white sharks (above).*

THE SKIES AND SPACE

The Earth is swathed in a thick, protective atmosphere. But objects from outer space regularly penetrate it, creating natural fireworks and other spectacular displays. They are reminders that Earth is a minute part of a dynamic universe.

From the beginning of time, people have turned their eyes to the heavens in a search for signs and omens to warn them of impending events. And very often nature has served up appropriate spectacles: shooting stars, comets, rainbows, eclipses of the Sun or Moon, mirages, and thunder and lightning – each phenomenon interpreted as a message from the gods, a foreboding of doom or, perhaps, of a happier event.

Often, the displays people see are not taking place millions of miles away in space, but in the atmosphere above their heads. This protective envelope of gas is able to bend and filter light, producing all manner of strange colours and optical distortions. There are, for example, the blue and green flashes sometimes seen at sunset. The beauty of the green flash impressed the French writer Jules Verne who wrote of it in 1882: 'If there is green in Paradise, it must be this green: the true green of hope.'

The atmosphere also acts as a barrier to rocks falling from space. Instead of landing on our heads, they burn up. As they do so, they often provide spectacular natural firework displays. One extraordinary event took place in 1933 and was seen over most of North America. First, a fiery red object with a long tail moved horizontally across the sky, followed shortly by 30 or 40 more in groups of three or four, aligned like aircraft flying in formation. Accompanying them were loud, thunder-like booms. They were meteors that had skimmed the atmosphere for over 6000 miles (9600 km) before burning up in the atmosphere.

THUNDER AND LIGHTNING

THE AWESOME POWERS OF NATURE THAT ENERGISE THE EARTH

Meteorologists estimate that 50 000 thunderstorms occur every day throughout the globe. According to another estimate, lightning flashes across the Earth are generating a constant output of some 4 billion kilowatts.

Typically, a thunderstorm begins on a late summer's day when the air is humid and the Sun is still burning hot in the afternoon. The moist air, warmed by the Sun-heated ground, rises, cools and condenses to form a cumulus cloud. If the heat from the ground is strong enough, the air carries on rising and the cloud grows higher and higher in the atmosphere. Eventually, the top of the cloud hits the top of the troposphere, the layer of the atmosphere that reaches to about 9 miles (15 km) above the Earth's surface. Here, the cloud spreads out to form the anvil-shaped head of a cumulonimbus or thundercloud, a huge thermodynamic machine with fast-moving air currents circulating within it. An electrical charge builds up on the ice

PLUNGING THROUGH EARTH'S ATMOSPHERE

Ionosphere
The upper atmosphere, or ionosphere, reaches from 53 miles (85 km) above Earth's surface to over 560 miles (900 km).

Mesosphere
This layer lies 31 to 53 miles (50 to 85 km) above Earth's surface.

Stratosphere
This extends from 9 to 31 miles (15 to 50 km) above Earth's surface. Ozone in this layer absorbs much of the Sun's ultra-violet radiation.

Troposphere
This layer extends up to 9 miles (15 km) above Earth's surface. Weather forms in this layer.

Aurora
A waving incandescent curtain of light forms when solar particles collide with air molecules in the upper atmosphere.

Meteorite
A lump of rock enters the atmosphere and burns up leaving a shining trail, sometimes called a shooting star.

IN FROM SPACE *Objects from space meet Earth's atmosphere and create natural fireworks.*

LIGHT FORKS OVER THE CITY *Lightning streaks across the night sky from clouds containing huge charges of electricity.*

METEORIC FALL *A shooting star dives across the sky. It is a fragment of matter from space, burning up as it reaches Earth's atmosphere.*

particles and water droplets inside the cloud whirled around by the air currents. This turns the cloud into a massive electric cell, with a positive charge at the top, and a negative one at the bottom.

The result is dramatic: a cloud which has the electrical force of several hundred million volts. The electricity may be discharged in a variety of ways, most usually from the negatively charged base of the cloud down to the positively charged ground (as forked lightning) or from the base up inside the cloud to the positively charged top (sheet lightning). The lightning heats the air to temperatures that approach 10 000°C (18 000°F). The sudden expansion of the heated air is heard a few seconds later as thunder.

SHOOTING STARS

TRAILS OF LOOSE MATTER
HURTLE THROUGH SPACE

There is still plenty of loose matter hurtling around the Sun, as well as the planets and their moons. Some of it is in clusters of asteroids – thousands of bodies orbiting the Sun, mostly between Mars and Jupiter, though some have orbits that intersect with the Earth's. The largest is Ceres, about 625 miles (1000 km) in diameter. The smallest known asteroids are only a few hundred yards across, and there are probably huge numbers of much smaller ones.

Occasionally, chunks of asteroids hit Earth, though most burn up by friction as they speed through the air. If a fragment reaches Earth, it is known as a meteorite. Other, smaller bodies also collide with Earth. As many as a billion dust grains from the tails of comets may enter the atmosphere in one day. At night, the glowing trail of debris that is left when one of these tiny grains burns up is briefly visible as a meteoroid – often called a 'shooting' or 'falling' star. In a dark country area you may see several an hour.

At certain times of the year, showers of shooting stars appear. They are thought to be fragments of comets still orbiting the Sun or long since disintegrated. Travelling up to 45 miles (72 km) per second, even a grain of dust can do serious damage to a spacecraft or satellite. However, the atmosphere shields us so efficiently that there is no example in recorded history of a human being hurt by a falling star.

STREAMS OF LIGHT

POLAR LIGHT-PLAY GENERATED BY THE
SUN'S ENERGY AND EARTH'S MAGNETISM

In the distant past, when Europe's skies were unpolluted by industrial emissions, the northern lights were sometimes seen as far south as Greece and Italy. Nowadays, you have to be somewhere near the North or South Poles, where they are generated,

NORTHERN LIGHTS *The aurora borealis shimmers on the Alaskan skyline.*

TINY HEART *The icy heart of a comet is tiny compared with its tail.*

the 'tail', sometimes hundreds of thousands of miles long, is in fact blown away from the comet by a 'solar wind' of particles escaping from the Sun.

One of the natural mysteries of the 20th century happened at Tunguska in Siberia. An object from space exploded with the force of a 15-megaton nuclear device over an uninhabited region of the province in 1908, razing trees across an area of some 3000 sq miles (7800 km^2). It left no crater, and no remains were found until an expedition in 1961 recovered tiny carbonaceous particles from the region. The body may have been a fragment of a comet no more than 22-65 yd (20-60 m) in diameter that blew itself apart in the upper atmosphere. A witness over 90 miles (150 km) away saw it in its dying seconds as a brilliant white mass looking larger than the Moon.

DARKNESS AT NOON

WHEN THE MOON BLACKS OUT
THE LIGHT OF THE SUN

In the Old Testament, God threatens the prophet Amos: 'I will cause the Sun to go down at noon, and I will darken the Earth in the clear day.' What he was threatening,

to appreciate the full splendour of the northern lights (aurora borealis) and their southern equivalent, the aurora australis. They are spectacular displays of blue, green, red, yellow or violet fire invading the sky in brilliant flashes, arcs and curtains and then fading just as suddenly.

The magic of the aurora is the result of streams of particles from the Sun. These are attracted towards the polar regions by the Earth's magnetic field, and when they strike the upper atmosphere they make it glow with the colours characteristic to its different gases. Green light is thus due to oxygen, red to nitrogen and blue to neon. A particularly bright aurora is usually the result of a flare on the Sun, which is often associated with a large sunspot.

SPACE TRAVELLERS

COMETS LEAVE SPECTACULAR
'BURNING' TAILS ACROSS THE SKY

To the ancients, comets were omens of great events – battles, disasters, the death of kings. Some comets appear regularly and are predictable, while others – usually the most spectacular – turn up from the depths of space with no warning. Comets run the gauntlet of gravitational pulls from the planets and asteroids, as well as from

the Sun itself. Thus, their route is never the same when they pass again.

The British astronomer Edmond Halley first realised that comets might travel in regular cycles when he calculated that the comet he observed in 1682 was the same one studied by Johannes Kepler in 1608 and Peter Apian in 1531. He predicted that it would return in 1758 or 1759 – which it did.

Modern studies have proved that comets are essentially 'dirty snowballs' consisting of 90 per cent ice and rich in carbon, hydrogen, nitrogen and oxygen, with some solid matter. Once they are close enough to the Sun, the outer layer of ice, gas and dust boils and becomes visible. The dust shines in the light of the Sun, and is radiant enough to be seen at vast distances. The nucleus of Halley's Comet may be no more than 12^1/$_2$ miles (20 km) across, but it is still visible more than 62 million miles (100 million km) away. The cloud of material known as

TOTAL ECLIPSE *This eclipse of the Sun was photographed in Mexico in March 1970.*

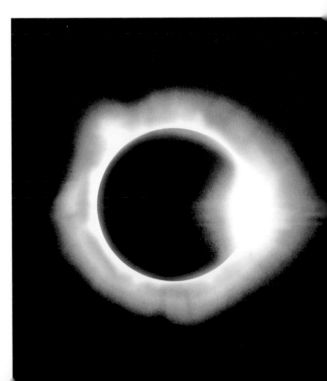

in fact, was a solar eclipse, when the Moon comes between the Earth and the Sun. During a total eclipse the sky darkens, colours fade, stars appear, and the temperature may plunge dramatically.

Armed with the right equipment during a total eclipse, it is possible to see flames and explosions leaping a good 250 000 miles (400 000 km) above the surface of the Sun. Normally it is extremely dangerous to observe the Sun directly; only when its bright surface is completely hidden by the Moon during a total eclipse can you enjoy the spectacle in safety.

A solar eclipse is always a localised phenomenon, since the Moon's shadow is less than 190 miles (300 km) wide, and both the Earth and Moon are constantly in motion. A total lunar eclipse – when the Earth casts its shadow on the Moon, thus blocking out its light – can be much longer, up to 100 minutes. This is because the Earth is large enough to cast a broader shadow than its satellite planet.

Solar and lunar eclipses happen in a cycle of just over 18 years – known as a 'saros', from an ancient Babylonian word for an astronomical cycle. Ten of the 41 solar eclipses in a saros will be total and 14 will be partial. The remaining 17 eclipses are 'annular' ones (from the Latin *anulus*, 'ring'), when instead of being completely covered by the disc of the Moon, the Sun's edges can be glimpsed as a brilliant ring of light shining out around the Moon's circumference.

Many planets in the solar system have moons that sometimes come between them and the Sun. Earth, however, benefits from a cosmic accident that makes its solar eclipses exceptionally spectacular. Not only is the Sun's diameter 400 times greater than the Moon's, but the Moon is 400 times closer to Earth than the Sun is. This means that both are able at precisely the right moments to cast the other into complete shadow. From Earth, this is a

FELL FROM THE SKY   The Chupaderos meteorite landed in northern Mexico and weighs over 8¹/₂ tons.

rare chance to see the faint outer atmosphere of the Sun – the 'corona' – normally too faint to be seen, though its temperature is well over 1 000 000°C (1 800 000°F).

STONES FROM OUTER SPACE

ROCKS THAT TURN TO DUST AS THEY

FLASH TOWARDS THE EARTH

Scientists estimate that something in the order of 40 000 tons of matter falls to Earth from space every year – more than 100 tons a day. Most of it burns up in the Earth's atmosphere to float down harmlessly as dust, but several thousand incoming objects survive the burning and come

to Earth weighing 2 lb (1 kg) or more. Some are pure metal – mostly iron or nickel; others are stone, or a mixture of stone and metal.

On August 12, 1993, a stone weighing over 18 lb (8 kg) landed in a garden in eastern France. On October 9, 1992, a 29 lb (13 kg) stone hit the back of an aging car in a New York suburb, and promptly raised its value. Almost exactly 500 years earlier, on November 16, 1492, a much larger stone weighing 280 lb (127 kg) fell from the skies

WHERE DO COMETS COME FROM?

How is it that new comets suddenly appear as if from nowhere? The answer lies at the fringes of the solar system in the form of icy material that was never swept up to become one of the giant outer planets, just as asteroids remain as rocky material that failed to make an additional inner planet. Perhaps as many as 1000 billion chunks of this primitive material remain beyond the orbit of Pluto, far outside the area of planetary formation. They survive in the form of the Oort Cloud – a spherical

shell of comet-like bodies named after the Dutch scientist Jan Hendrik Oort who first suggested that it might exist.

The Oort Cloud has a total mass estimated at the equivalent of about 100 Earths, and a diameter of about 100 000 AU. One AU, or 'astronomical unit', is the mean distance between the Earth and the Sun, about 93 million miles (150 million km).

Because comets lose mass each time they venture close enough to the Sun, it has been

estimated that no comet could survive more than about 100 visits. They would either break up, shrink into insignificance, or perhaps be 'captured' by a planet or the Sun. But new comets continue to appear, so we must suppose that something happens to shake them out of storage in the Oort Cloud and divert them through the solar system.

The current explanation is that they are dislodged by gravitational forces exerted by passing stars, or pulled by the great mass of one of our outer planets.

at Ensisheim in Alsace. For many years it was kept in the local parish church, and its remains can still be seen in the town hall. It is the oldest meteorite still preserved, with records describing when it fell.

The world's largest known meteorite to survive intact fell in prehistoric times in the area of modern Namibia, and weighs about 60 tons; it can still be seen.

Nothing so heavy seems to have fallen to Earth in the few thousand years of recorded human history, but in Arabia, Argentina, Canada, Germany, the United States and elsewhere, craters measuring up to 62 miles (100 km) across mark places where huge meteorites have evidently landed in the distant past.

Astronomers have calculated that about once a century, a meteorite measuring 30 ft (10 m) across strikes the Earth with an impact equivalent to that of the Hiroshima A-bomb – that is, about 20 000 tons of TNT or one-fiftieth of a megaton. Further calculations suggest that Earth must also be hit by as many as six meteorites with a diameter of 5/8 mile (1 km) every million years, and by one or two meteorites with a diameter of just over 6 miles (10 km) every 100 million years.

The last would strike with the energy of 100 million one-megaton H-bombs. It would blast a crater 62 miles (100 km) across, cause earthquakes and tidal waves on a titanic scale across the globe, strew burning debris for thousands of miles around, and fill the atmosphere with enough acids and dust to cause severe acid rainstorms and months of near darkness.

Scientists have even tried to attribute some of the colossal extinctions that have been a feature of Earth's history to impacts of this kind. The disappearance, for example, of the dinosaurs about 65 million years ago may have been triggered by a 6 mile (10 km) astroid that fell as a meteorite, possibly in the Caribbean region.

THE WONDER OF RAINBOWS

CREATION'S COLOURS SEEN THROUGH
A SCREEN OF RAINDROPS

In Greek and Roman mythology, Iris, the goddess of the rainbow – whose name appears in the word 'iridescent' – was one of the messengers of the gods, possibly because her rainbow symbol stretched from heaven to Earth. In Irish legend, leprechauns are supposed to bury their pots of gold where the rainbow ends – a place forever safe from humans, since by their very nature rainbows can only be seen at a distance.

In 1666, the English scientist Isaac Newton observed that by passing the white light of the Sun through a glass prism, he could split it into the colours of the rainbow: red, orange, yellow, green, blue, indigo, violet. A raindrop can produce the same effect. Visible light is part of a band of electromagnetic radiation – similar to radio waves – with wavelengths that

UNDER THE RAINBOW *To see a*
rainbow, you have to have the
Sun behind you, with rain still
falling in front. The raindrops
reflect and refract the light
(top) to paint one of nature's
most brilliant pictures.

range from very long to very short. Every different wavelength of light has its own colour. Although the wavelengths enter a prism – or raindrop – together as 'white' light, it bends, or refracts, each wavelength at a slightly different angle, so that it leaves the prism as an individual colour. These colours range across the spectrum from red to violet.

In the same way, light enters a raindrop and is refracted. But with a raindrop, it is then reflected from the back of the drop – which acts like a mirror – and is refracted once more as it leaves. The light thus bounces back out, but leaves the raindrop in a slightly different direction from that at which it entered. The violet wavelength comes out at the highest level of the spectrum, the red wavelength comes out at the lowest.

When this happens inside millions of raindrops simultaneously, each raindrop is reflecting a slightly different wavelength back to observers. They can see the violet wavelengths from the lower drops, but the red wavelengths from the same drops are being reflected too low to reach them.

HOW RAINBOWS ARE FORMED

Water prisms
Raindrops act like prisms to reflect and refract the sunlight.

Viewing position
Sunlight shines from behind the observer and is reflected back to him or her as a rainbow.

Conversely, the higher raindrops reflect their violet wavelengths too high for observers to see them, but their red wavelengths are visible. The result is a rainbow of seven different colours – red on the upper outer edge, then passing through the entire spectrum to reach a band of violet on the inner edge.

The colours appear in an arc, instead of a straight line, because it is only along an arc that light is refracted from the raindrops at the appropriate angle for it to be seen by the observer.

Sometimes, you can see a 'secondary' paler-coloured rainbow – as opposed to the other 'primary' one. It appears because some of the light that enters a raindrop is reflected not once but twice from the back of the drop before it leaves. It loses a degree of light in the process and there-fore appears fainter. Moreover, because the light has been reflected twice within the raindrop, the emerging colours come out in reverse order.

To see a rainbow, three conditions are needed:

1 It must still be raining in the sector of the sky that is opposite to the Sun. Only when the Sun is behind you can you see the light reflected.

2 The Sun must not be too high in the sky. If it is, the reflected light cannot reach the observer on the ground.

3 Raindrops must be large enough to refract the colours clearly. A rainbow produced by drizzle – with raindrops less than 1/8 in (4 mm) across – will be nearly white, known as a 'fogbow'. The large rain-drops in a thunderstorm create a rainbow with bright, distinct bands of colour.

In the tropics, where early evening downpours are common, the rainbow is considered a serpent that swallows the rain. Elsewhere in the world, it also has spiritual or legendary significance. It is the bridge used by soul 'boats' in Indonesia. Arabs and the Bantu people of Africa believe the rainbow to be a divine bow for firing arrows; the Masai of East Africa think of it as the cloak of god. In Christian tradi-tion, the rainbow has often represented the throne of Christ.

OPTICAL ILLUSIONS SUSPENDED IN THE SKY

BENT LIGHT PROJECTING DECEIVING
MIRAGES ABOVE THE HORIZON

Sailors may see a ship afloat in the sky, while travellers in the Sahara may come upon a palm-fringed lake in the open desert – neither of which really exists.

Although these mirages are optical illusions, they are not delusions – they can be photographed. They are the result of refraction that bends light not only when it passes through a prism, but whenever it passes from any medium to another of a

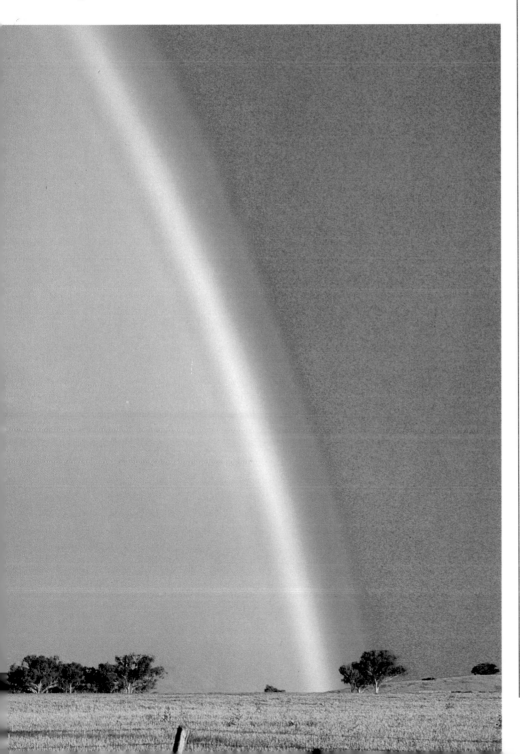

HEAVENLY BRIDGE *Many traditional beliefs see the rainbow as a bridge between the gods and men.*

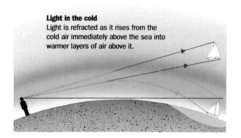

Light in the cold
Light is refracted as it rises from the cold air immediately above the sea into warmer layers of air above it.

FALSE PROMISE *The cold seas off north Germany are ideal territory for mirages, such as this one of buildings. Mirages form where light is refracted as it passes from hot air to cooler, denser air above it (left), or from cold air up into hotter air (right).*

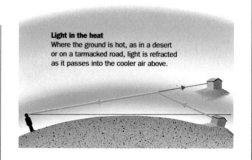

Light in the heat
Where the ground is hot, as in a desert or on a tarmacked road, light is refracted as it passes into the cooler air above.

different density. For example, it is refraction that causes a straight stick to look crooked when you put half of it in water, and similarly, it makes fish look closer to the surface of a river or stream than they really are.

Light can also be refracted inside a single medium if that medium contains layers of different densities. In the case of air, this is likely to happen above an unusually hot or unusually cold surface, because hot air expands to become less dense than cold air. The greater the difference in temperature between the two layers, the greater the chance of unusual optical effects.

There are two main types of mirage. The first type can be seen in hot regions, or wherever a hot Sun beats on a heat-

retaining surface – a road, say, or a sandy beach. When light rays from an object beyond the horizon slant down into a layer of hotter air, they may be refracted roughly parallel to the ground. The result is that a distant observer sees them as if the object were standing in a shimmering pool. When light from the sky hits a ground-level layer of hot air, it may be refracted as a silvered shimmering pool, looking more like a sheet of mercury than water.

The second type of mirage happens in colder regions, above ice sheets or freezing seas where, reversing the usual pattern, it is the air closest to the ground that is coldest, and the layer above it relatively warm. Here, light rays travelling upwards through the cold meet a warmer layer that bends them down again. An observer sees

the image of a boat or perhaps of a whole island apparently suspended in the sky. In both kinds of mirage, the distant object may be refracted upside down. Sometimes these variations in the density of air produce an effect called 'looming' where a scene beyond the horizon is not only made visible but is also magnified.

Tricks of refraction have given rise to some extraordinary mirages. In 1955, the crew of a ship that was steaming off Cape Finisterre in north-western Spain saw two suns, one above the other, at sunset. An unusual 'lateral' mirage observed at sea in 1957 produced two suns side by side.

Another extraordinary 'mirage' is the 'Silent City of Alaska', said to appear every year on the Mount Fairweather glacier on the border between Alaska and Canada,

SHADOW MOUNTAIN *A setting Sun projects the shadow of Mauna Kea in Hawaii.*

and was first reported in the British Royal Meteorological Society's *Quarterly Journal* in 1901. It occurs between 7 and 9 o'clock, between June 21 and July 10, and seems to show the buildings of a city. Some people have even identified these with buildings in Bristol, England, sited about 2500 miles (4020 km) away, claiming that the church tower of St Mary Redcliffe is clearly visible.

A similar 'mirage' is of a city seen on the Straits of Messina between Sicily and Italy. In fact, both are examples of 'fata morgana', a name derived from Morgan le Fay, King Arthur's enchantress sister, whose magic was able to make a city of towering castles and spires appear in the sky and lure seafarers to a watery death. In scientific terms, a fata morgana is a trick of the light that makes details on the horizon stretch upwards, so that they look like the spires and towers of a distant city.

A GIANT SHADOW IN THE SKY

A MOMENT AT DAWN WHEN THE EARTH'S SHADOW SHOWS

In countryside where the skies are clear and the horizon bare, you can often catch sight of an 'arch' before dawn. To see it at its best, you have to rise early and look in the direction exactly opposite to where the Sun will rise. Before dawn, when the sky begins to brighten, watch for the appearance of a long grey curve that will slowly dwindle and then vanish the moment the Sun appears. This phenomenon is the shadow of the Earth being briefly cast by the Sun on the atmosphere.

Another unusual shadow can be seen from the summit of an isolated mountain, such as Pico de Tiede, highest point in the Canary Islands. At sunrise on a clear morning, the dark pyramid-like shadow of the volcano extends 124 miles (200 km) out to sea, making it one of the longest shadows cast in the world.

NIGHT-SHINING CLOUDS HIGH ABOVE THE EARTH

ICE-CLAD METEORITE DUST THAT GLOWS AFTER SUNSET

Between 43 and 60 miles (70 and 90 km) above the Earth's surface the atmosphere contains clouds known as 'noctilucent' – night-shining. Scientists believe that they consist of microscopic ice-clad dust particles, probably left over from meteorite trails. Because they occur at such great heights, they do not affect the climate and weather we experience in the lower atmosphere.

Most clouds do not reach higher than 10 miles (16 km) above the Earth.

In the way that a mountain peak or high-flying aircraft can stay visible long after the Sun has set at ground level, so these noctilucent clouds are high enough to shine with the Sun's reflected light by night. They appear as vast formations, sometimes a brilliant blue or silver colour, sometimes yellow or red, but only in the summer months at latitudes above 45° north and south.

HEAVENLY HALOS

RAINBOW RINGS THAT CENTRE AROUND THE SUN AND MOON

One of the rarest of rainbow-like displays is a circular one that sometimes appears around the Sun with colours, weaker than in an ordinary rainbow, banded red to violet from inside to outside. It is seen when the sky is veiled by a thin layer of cirrus or cirrostratus – high-level clouds made up of ice crystals that are able to diffract light much as a prism does. Sometimes, a second 'large ring' (as opposed to the inner 'small ring') will form around the same centre – as happens sometimes with rainbows – with the colours in it reversed. Halos are also sometimes seen around the Moon, though these are never coloured.

Halos or arcs are produced by sunlight or moonlight that has been reflected or refracted – or both – by ice crystals formed

NIGHT-SHINING *The glowing mass of a noctilucent cloud hangs over a night-time Finnish skyline.*

CROWN OF LIGHT *An eclipse of the Sun creates a large round halo of light.*

at altitudes ranging from 20 000 to 30 000 ft (6000 to 10 000 m) above the surface of the Earth. Like a kind of giant chandelier, the ice crystals bend and split the light, the shape of the halo determined by the dimensions of the crystals. Sometimes ice crystals split the image of the Sun to create two small luminous spots on either side of it, known as parhelia ('mock suns' or 'sundogs'). The same phenomenon can happen with the Moon to create paraslenae ('mock moons').

Another kind of luminous ring, the 'corona', is sometimes visible around the Sun or Moon, but also forms around other brilliant bodies such as the planets Venus or Jupiter, or the star Sirius. Unlike the other rings, the corona appears to touch the body it encircles. Sometimes, a corona appears when stratus cloud has formed near the Sun, Moon or other body. Stratus clouds are grey layer clouds which occur at heights of less than 1000 ft (300 m) above the Earth's surface and contain not ice crystals but water droplets. These diffract the light and produce a yellowish corona that is usually edged with fuzzy red.

The colour of a halo varies according to the shape and even the altitude of the falling ice crystals that reflect or diffract its source of light. The size of a corona depends upon the size of the droplets that cause it: the smaller the droplets the broader the corona.

In high latitudes, lunar halos are often seen after a display of the northern or southern lights. Large corona displays are often associated with volcanic eruptions. An example of one of these displays, known as Bishop's Ring – after one of the people who studied it, in Honolulu – was seen in the dust from the spectacular eruption of Krakatoa in 1883. It appeared as a blue inner circle and a reddish-brown outer circle around the Sun. This was unusual, because normal halos have the red portion of the ring on the inside. Bishop's Ring is thought to form at high altitudes, at least 50 miles (80 km) above the Earth's surface.

Not all halos are simple circles. An unusual solar halo was seen from the north Italian coast at midday in June 1954. A dark, blue-grey disc appeared around the

Sun, followed by another to the right. The circumference of both discs contained concentric rings coloured like the rainbow. Another spectacular halo of concentric rings was seen in the United States in 1841. The phenomenon consisted of three to five circular zones of light, the innermost glowing like the most brilliant rainbow. Inside the halo, the Sun was swathed in what was described as a dense vapour. What made this halo different from any that had been seen before or since was the presence of another circle and a stacked series of overlapping pure white arcs of circles to the right of the Sun.

Halos are not always circular. Elliptical halos have been seen around the Moon, and in 1913 observers on board the RMS *Balmoral Castle* off West Africa saw a square lunar halo. The Moon was framed in a

---

THE SOUNDS OF WEATHER

Nature has its mysterious sounds as well as its spectacular lights and colours. Just before a thunderstorm, a sizzling or crackling sound warns of an imminent lightning strike, given off by electrical discharges from pointed objects. Certain hills make a hollow moaning sound when the wind blows, probably because they behave like gigantic organ pipes, whereas tornadoes scream like the noise of freight trains or jet aircraft. And when snow is trodden on, it makes a higher-pitched sound the colder the weather is because the snow crystals become more and more brittle.

---

dull, yellowish square halo, about three times the diameter of the Moon, with one corner of the square pointing down towards the horizon.

Remember, direct sunlight will damage your eyes, so take precautions when you observe halos or atmospheric effects around the Sun.

MARVELS 3 OF THE PLANT WORLD

ORANGE-PEEL PEZIZA *This fungus mimics the colour of orange peel and the white pith.*

PLANTS ARE EVERYWHERE. THROUGHOUT THE WORLD, FROM THE LOFTIEST TROPICAL FORESTS TO THE SKIMPIEST SUB-ARCTIC TUNDRA COVER, IN DESERTS, RAIN FORESTS, GRASSLANDS AND WETLANDS, IN THE SEA AND ON THE MOUNTAINS AND ICE SHEETS, THE EARTH IS CLOAKED IN A MOSAIC OF VEGETATION. AND WHEREVER PLANTS GROW, HOW THEY GROW IS LINKED TO CLIMATE. EARLY IN THEIR EVOLUTION PLANTS WERE AT THE MERCY OF WIND, ICE AND WATER. BUT AFTER MILLIONS OF YEARS OF DEVELOPMENT AND ADAPTATION THEY HAVE CONQUERED THE ELEMENTS. THE RESULT IS A KINGDOM OF BIZARRE SHAPES AND STRUCTURES, WITH MANY INGENIOUS MECHANISMS FOR REPRODUCTION AND DISPERSAL.

PASSIONFLOWER *An everyday beauty of the American tropics.*

STRANGE PROFILES

Plants grow in many inhospitable places – from deserts, to mountaintops, to salt marshes. But to survive in them, they have had to evolve shapes and structures that cope with drought, frost or a twice-daily ducking in sea water.

Nature is at the same time architect, civil engineer, designer and builder. And as plants have evolved, they have recognised all the rules of hydraulics and of building mechanics. The result is that species exist that are equipped to survive just about anywhere on Earth.

People in hot countries, for example, have long known that the sphere, with the smallest possible surface area in proportion to its mass, is the best shape to reduce the rate at which heat is absorbed and water evaporated, and so many buildings in such countries have domed roofs. The same principle is at work in nature, so that many desert plants are globular. In this way, half the plant is always in the shade.

Nature also pre-empted the tinted window of office blocks. The African desert plant *Fenestraria* grows mostly below ground with only a window of translucent cells at the surface. Some of the cells filter out dangerous ultraviolet light, while others diffuse the bright desert light to manageable levels for photosynthesis – by which green plants turn light into energy.

Cactuses, by contrast, stand above ground, growing to tremendous sizes. To store the water they need to survive in hot deserts, they must have a strong cage-like structure, with a pliable, pleated outer skin to contain and support the weight of the water. The reinforced-concrete structure of modern buildings is based on exactly the same principle.

LIVING FOSSIL

A DESERT DWARF THAT CAN THRIVE FOR UP TO 2000 YEARS

The dwarf tree *Welwitschia mirabilis* has one of the most unusual designs in the plant world. With an iron-hard stem rarely more than knee-high to a human, but up to 5 ft (1.5 m) in diameter, the tree has two long leaves that sprout from the base at a rate of 6 in (15 cm) a year. They can be up to 30 ft (9 m) long, writhing across the ground, torn by winds and fraying at the ends, so that in time they form a tangled mass that might well cover an area of about 200 sq ft (20 m²). Up to 9 ft (2.7 m) of the stem, meanwhile, lies underground, and the tap root reaches still deeper.

A young *Welwitschia* may be a few hundred years old; an

ENTRENCHED *The dwarf tree* Welwitschia *can survive for centuries in the parched wastes of the Namib Desert.*

old one may date from the time of Christ, 2000 years ago. *Welwitschia* is a species that also has separate male and female plants, bearing cones similar to flowers. It is adapted to thrive in one of the world's most hostile regions, the Namib Desert of Namibia, where the average rainfall is less than $1/2$ in (1.3 cm) a year and five years may pass without rain. It never grows more than 62 miles (100 km) from the Atlantic Ocean, and has evolved a survival strategy quite unlike that of most desert plants, which tend to rely for their water on elaborate root systems.

In addition to what it can get from its long tap root, the plant's pores absorb water from the heavy morning fogs that cling to the Namibian coast and are often blown inland. When the Sun disperses the fog, the pores close to retain the water.

The seeds have to wait for the desert's occasional rainfall before they can germinate. Here, too, *Welwitschia* is specialised for arid conditions. In most plants the 'cotyledons' – the first leaves of the embryo seed – are discarded after a few days. *Welwitschia* has cotyledons that store enough food reserves to continue feeding the young plant for up to five years, until the next rainfall arrives.

COLOSSAL CACTUS

MEXICO'S SAGUARO CACTUS IS A STANDING WATER RESERVOIR

The saguaro, or giant cactus (*Carnegiea gigantea*), is the strongest, most massive plant that grows in the Arizona and Sonora deserts of the United States and Mexico. Its silhouette is familiar from a hundred Westerns, a fluted column up to 50 ft (15 m) tall and 28 in (70 cm) across, sometimes an isolated figure, and often with arms reaching skyward.

The saguaro starts its life as a single stem that may wait till it is 75 years old and 16 to 26 ft (5 to 8 m) tall before it produces its first side branches. These sprout horizontally but soon turn upwards to grow more or less parallel with the main stem. It is this slow and regular habit of growth that gives veteran saguaros two or three

centuries old their majestic outlines and stately presence.

In order to grow in this harsh environment, the giant has developed several strategies. As well as a main tap root, it anchors itself to the ground with thick lateral roots that go little more than 3 ft (about 1 m) deep and a system of shallow rootlets that radiate in a circle 100 ft (30 m) across to

STANDING RESERVOIR *The tall fluted columns of the saguaro can store many gallons of water.*

mop up every drop of rainfall. After a fairly humid summer it may weigh up to 6 or 7 tons, 75 per cent of it water. In this way, it accumulates and stores enough water to last it for two years of total drought, by

GHOST OF THE DESERT

The desert amaranth, *Amaranthus graecizans*, is one of the tumbleweeds seen clambering over the sidewalks and porches of lonely ghost towns in traditional American Westerns. This apparently aimless wanderer is using a survival strategy particularly well designed for the vast open spaces of North America, and one practised by several plant families on the other steppes and prairies of the world.

The amaranth is an annual that is green and well rooted in summer but withers completely in the cold and

drought of autumn. It dries into a ball of tangled branches that detaches itself from the root to embark on a wind-borne career that may take it hundreds of miles away. But the ball is not just a travelling skeleton looking for a grave: it carries a supply of seeds, and sows them as it rolls.

PLAINS DRIFTER *Balls of tumbleweed scatter seeds along their random trail.*

---

which time its girth will probably have halved.

The saguaro's large flowers yield red fruits or 'apples' full of small black seeds. Botanists have worked out that in the course of a century this cactus can produce 40 million seeds, of which only three or four are likely to reach maturity – a loss rate that is due partly to the harsh conditions and partly to the many animals that take a liking to the apples' sweet and juicy flesh. Humans also play their part by eating the fruit pulp raw or stewed, or by fermenting it to make alcoholic drinks, known as *mescal* or *tequila*.

FLOWERING PHOENIX

VETERAN GRASS TREES ABLE TO SURVIVE AND EXPLOIT BUSH FIRES

The native Australian yacca plant, or *Xanthorrhoea preissii*, is known for the characteristic colour of its massive flame-seared trunk, crowned by wiry tufts of foliage. Like its distant cousins the yuccas

THRIVING ON FIRE *Fires only encourage the grass tree to sprout and flower.*

and agaves of the Americas, this unique plant, which is found only in south-western Australia, prefers semi-arid regions. Yaccas grow slowly, live for at least 350 years, and have the special ability not only to resist and survive the bush fires common in such habitats, but also to exploit them.

Another name for this plant is the grass tree. After a bush fire has died, the top foliage singed by flames is quickly replaced by new shoots, while the remains of the old leaves surround and protect the trunk and bulk it out. Just as grasses in savannah country survive, so grass trees are stimulated by scorching, their height depending more on the number of bush fires they have lived through than on their age. It seems that their flowering is also triggered by the heat of flames, since those that grow near inhabited areas, where fires are more prevalent, bloom more often than their relatives in the wild.

DESERT 'CANDLES' FULL OF WATER

THE CALIFORNIAN TREE THAT CAN BE A LIFE-SAVER IN DROUGHT

In the United States and Mexico, the *Fouquieria columnaris* tree is known as the 'cirio' – Spanish for 'candle'. It is an appropriate image, for its trunk really does resemble a giant altar candle, gradually tapering from the base, which may be up to 3 ft (roughly 1 m) in diameter, to heights of 60 ft (18 m). Short, spiny branches spiral

up its trunk, and near the top often grow out and up in a dense tangle. Early injuries caused by the wind may deform these topmost branches into grotesquely writhing shapes.

The cirio bristles with spines that deter browsing herbivores. Its miniature leaves also sprout close to the trunk, and present so small a surface to the Sun that the plant is rarely affected by high temperatures.

SPIKY CANDLE *Thorns and a waxy coat protect the cirio.*

Both trunk and branches are covered with a thick waxy bark whose pores close up in excessive heat to protect their pulpy inner tissues. These hold so much water that ranchers will fell them during droughts to feed their cattle.

With adaptations like these, the plant has become one of the most successful inhabitants of the Vizcaino-Magdalena desert of Baja California, growing in forests towering above most other desert vegetation, which tends to hug the ground. When rains permit, its tubular pale yellow flowers appear in early summer perched at the very top of the slender trunk.

STUBBORN ANDEAN SURVIVOR

A COUSIN OF THE PINEAPPLE LIVES FOR 100 YEARS, BLOSSOMS ONCE AND DIES

At an altitude of over 13 000 ft (4000 m) in the Andes of Peru and Bolivia grows the *Puya raimondii*, a stubborn member of the pineapple family, the bromeliads. At this height the range of temperature between night and day is huge, the nocturnal frost intense, and to escape the effects of fierce winds, few plants risk growing more than a few inches high.

Yet there in the Andes, where temperatures are nearly 27°C (80°F) lower than at sea level, the puya builds a trunk up to 8 ft (2.5 m) tall and 32 in (80 cm) wide. It is crowned with a bristling sphere of spiky leaves 47 in (1.2 m) long, and bordered by rows of hooked thorns designed to deter the most leather-lipped herbivore. Dead or alive, these leaves wrap the trunk in a thick layer that prevents the nourishing sap from freezing into lethal ice.

When – after about 100 years – the plant finally reaches maturity it sprouts, over a period of three months, a floral crown 13 to 20 ft (4 to 6 m) tall and consisting of several hundred branches curled tightly around a central spike that may

BOTANICAL EXCLAMATION MARK **Puya raimondii** *lives high in the Andes, and flowers only once during its lifetime.*

bear as many as 8000 flowers. When the flowers wither they release millions of seeds to scatter in the wind. Once it has perpetuated its species by this single burst of extravagant flowering, the plant dies.

IS IT A MAN . . . OR IS IT A PLANT?

A SLOW-GROWING SUCCULENT THAT STORES WATER FOR ITS SURVIVAL

The *Pachypodium namaquanum* has a bulbous base and narrow neck, and close up it looks rather like a wine bottle. In fact, it is filled with water: a very necessary reserve

supply, to keep the plant alive in regions where sometimes it rains only once every four or five years. In African legend, it is regarded as being half man, half plant – and its silhouette at a distance can indeed appear to be human.

Standing 8 to 16 ft (2.5 to 5 m) tall, the *Pachypodium namaquanum* grows only in the far south of the Namib Desert, on the frontier of South Africa and Namibia. Its bare upright trunk is covered in spines and has no branches except for a few short ones at the top, which produce leaves only at the tips.

Curiously, the head leans northward

TRESPASSERS BEWARE *The* namaquanum *is a thorny citizen of the Namib Desert.*

at an angle of between 20° and 30°, a characteristic shared by other slow-growing succulent plants, such as the euphorbias of South Africa. The *namaquanum* has thus earned itself the nickname of the 'magnetic plant' – as if it were a living compass. But the Earth's magnetic field has little to do with it. It seems more likely that because these plants live in the Southern Hemisphere, where the Sun lies northward, their stems simply lean towards the source of light.

The plant is now quite rare, restricted to an area in the Namib Desert known as the Richtersveld, where the only moisture available comes from dense fogs rolling in at night from the southern Atlantic Ocean. Its existence is threatened by plant collectors and the destruction of its habitat as a result of mineral prospecting and exploitation.

A THISTLE THAT LOOKS LIKE A MELON

A DOWNY CLOAK PROTECTS MELOCACTUS FLORETS FROM DEHYDRATION

Early in the Europeans' discovery of the New World, they encountered strange, rounded, bristling plants, which the German botanist Jakob Tabernaemontanus

MELON CACTUS *Brown caps top green stems in the* Melocactus communis.

described in 1588 as 'thistles that look like melons'. The plants were later christened melocactus, or melon cactus.

Also known as the 'Turk's cap cactus', the Jamaican *Melocactus communis* has a woolly flowering head with a characteristic that is unusual in the botanical world. When the seeds of the cactus germinate, they produce a fleshy, green and spiny

DESIGNER FUNGI

The flesh of some fungi can mould itself into an extraordinary range of shapes, from delicate frills and gills to spongy parasols, staghorns and puffballs. It can also form solid shelves or brackets so tough that you can stand on them.

Myriostoma coliforme looks like the lid of a pepper shaker set in the middle of a star. The small holes that perforate the central sphere allow the spores to escape; the sphere is attached to the star that bears it by several short feet. A variety of bizarre designs are found among the *Gasteromycetes*, the puffballs and their allies, some of them brightly coloured and foul-smelling.

Clathrus ruber, the red clathrus or

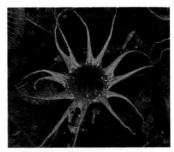

STINKHORN, *DICTYOPHORA* SP.

CAGE FUNGUS, *CLATHRUS RUBER*

STAR FUNGUS, *CLATHRUS* SP.

STINKHORN, *LATERNA PUSILLA*

cage fungus, first appears as a brown, egg-shaped body in the ground. It then bursts out of its package to expand and take the shape of a hollow pink or scarlet ball, with a series of rounded diamond shapes cut out of its surface. It grows up to 5 in (12 cm) across, and smells putrid enough to lure the flies that spread its pores.

Anthurus archeri develops the shape of a red star emerging from a sticky membranous bag at the centre. Both species arrived in temperate Europe hidden in the wool of sheep imported from Australia.

FRILLS AND STARS *Many fungi take strange and exotic forms.*

FORKING OUT Kokerboom trees spread out against the south-west African sky.

stalk that develops for five to ten years without flowering, and then stops growing. The head of the stalk produces a special organ, the cephalium, which may grow to be 3 ft (roughly 1 m) or more tall – it bears a passing resemblance to a fez, hence the name Turk's cap. Buds cluster all over it, and it also becomes covered with supple spines smaller than the ones on the stem. Some of these are transformed into a luxuriant downy fleece, while each bud produces a flower.

It is this flowering that makes the plant so special. Unlike other plants whose stems support and sustain the flowers, the stem of *Melocactus* soaks up water to feed the cephalium, which then flowers, bears fruit and perpetuates the species. The florets

are protected from dehydration by their fuzzy cloak of down, and as a further precaution open only at night to avoid being baked by the tropical Sun.

CROWNED HEADS OF THE AFRICAN DESERT

THE KOKERBOOM TREE WHOSE SWEET NECTAR IS A LURE TO BABOONS

What makes the kokerboom particularly remarkable is its ability to thrive in the most barren regions of south-west Africa – where no other tree can tolerate the hostile habitat. The *Aloe dichotoma*, or kokerboom, can be over 3 ft (1 m) in diameter at ground level, its tough smooth trunk gradually narrowing as it grows to reach a height of 23 ft (7 m). Halfway up, the trunk forks into two branches, each branch then dividing yet again and so on – a rare feature

among flowering plants. The tips of the branches finally develop rosettes of foliage. Through this pattern of recurring subdivision, the crown of the tree develops a distinctive dome shape.

The greyish-green halo of the foliage is splashed with bright yellow patches in June and July, when the nectar-rich flowers appear and the insects and birds come swarming around. Baboons are fond of kokerboom trees and have been known to strip them bare.

Although the tree appears tall and strong from a distance, closer inspection often reveals a spindly, peeling trunk that is streaked with white. The clubfoot is locked into the rocky ground with thin, fibrous roots. Nevertheless, a kokerboom will often survive in its wilderness site for 100 years or more, absorbing water from the sea mists that envelop it at night. Local

Hottentots and Bushmen have traditionally used the branches to make holders for their arrows and have given it the name 'quiver tree'.

TREES WITH ROOTS LIKE STILTS

AERIAL ROOTS ALLOW MANGROVE
TREES TO SURVIVE IN SWAMPS

The mangrove tree, *Rhizophora,* has a tangle of aerial roots that give it the air of a gigantic octopus squatting on the surface of a swamp. The roots grow out of its trunk, with the lower branches acting as stabilisers in the shifting mud of tropical shorelines

and tidal flats. When the tide ebbs, the roots are exposed above the water and absorb oxygen from the air, while the underground roots remain submerged.

Low tide reveals a dense scaffolding of impenetrable evergreen forest. These labyrinths provide shelter for creatures from oysters and sponges to shrimps and crabs. They are also nurseries for big sea-going fish, such as sharks and tarpon.

The mangrove reproduces in this water-logged environment by keeping its seeds out of the water. The fruit remains attached to the branches of the parent tree. The seed inside germinates in the damp air and puts out a single primary root that may

grow as much as 10 in (25 cm) long. When the seedling is ready, it detaches itself, drops into the water and, remaining upright, takes root in the muddy bottom.

THE TRAVELLER'S TREE

IT HAS A TRUNK LIKE A PALM TREE
AND LEAVES THAT STORE WATER

The *Ravenala madagascariensis* is a god-send to the thirsty, since it holds reservoirs of rainwater around its trunk – hence its

ROOTS IN THE AIR *Mangrove trees grow in salt water, and thus help to stabilise tropical shorelines.*

BOTANICAL WEATHER FORECASTERS

The rose of Jericho, *Anastatica hierochuntica*, is a member of the mustard family found in arid regions from Morocco and across North Africa to Syria and southern Iran. In dry weather it wilts, shrivels and appears dead. Then, in a spectacular resurrection, the stem fills out and turns green again. The plant is so sensitive that it is able to extract moisture from the humidity in the air when there is the slightest hint of rain.

ANASTATICA HIEROCHUNTICA

Another plant that reacts to the atmosphere is *Selaginella lepidophylla*. A fern growing on limestone slopes from the southern United States to Central America, the *Selaginella* curls up into a ball in dry weather, but unfolds into a green rosette when rain is in the air.

SELAGINELLA LEPIDOPHYLLA

more familiar name, the 'traveller's tree'. Specimens have been planted in gardens throughout the tropical world since the first Western travellers began to visit the island of Madagascar off south-eastern Africa in the 16th century.

The tree is a member of a banana-like family, the Strelitziaceae, confined to the rain forests of the east coast of Madagascar. The trunk looks, in fact, like a palm tree's, with a topknot of long leaves.

It is the arrangement of the leaves that makes it unique in the plant world. Leaves on most other plants occur in a pattern that spirals around the trunk and branches. *Ravenala* obeys this rule, but its leaves sprout at intervals of 180°, and so lie opposite each other along the trunk in a single vertical plane. Each of the ragged-edged leaves is attached to the trunk by a long stalk that ends in a kind of sheath with a

A FAN UNFURLED *The traveller's tree stores water at the base of each interlocking stem: a useful tip for parched travellers – hence its name.*

groove running into it. The sheaths overlap, leaving a closed space in between.

Rainwater runs down the leaves and stalks, which act like overflow pipes, and is stored in these natural reservoirs. The hanging pools built into *Ravenala*'s axils – the angle between stalk and trunk – are homes for all kinds of wildlife. They are watering places, too, for passing creatures, particularly many species of birds.

The axils also contain the tree's massive flower heads – clusters in which each flower may grow up to 10 in (25 cm) long. They produce black seeds, embedded in a fleshy blue fruit that is irresistible to birds, who eat the flesh and so disperse the seeds.

MODERATION AND EXCESS

The plant kingdom is full of superlatives and diminutives. The biggest single living thing on Earth, for example, is a plant. Named after the US soldier General William T. Sherman, it is a Californian redwood or giant sequoia, with a girth of 79 ft (24 m), a height of 260 ft (79 m) and an estimated weight of about 2000 tons. This enormous tree and others of the species, some smaller in girth but greater in height, are found in the temperate rain forests along the north-west coast of North America, notably in an impressive redwood grove in the Redwood Creek Valley in California. Among them is the 'Howard Libby' tree – a 367 ft (112 m) redwood giant – and there used to be others, known to have reached heights of 395 ft (120 m) or more.

In this coastal strip, known as the 'fog belt', to the west of the Rocky Mountains, conditions encourage trees to grow to a giant size. Onshore winds bring an abundance of water from the vast Pacific Ocean, and the deep, well-aerated soils are rich in all kinds of nutrients. Another product of this fertile land is the Douglas fir, which pushes its straight, cylindrical trunk over 330 ft (100 m) into the sky.

In the wet forests of eastern Australia, some species of eucalyptus grow to comparably monster proportions. The mountain ash, as it is known

LARGE AND LITTLE *A giant sequoia (left) towers into the air. Arctic willows (right), by contrast, never grow more than a few inches tall.*

locally in the state of Victoria, grows up to 330 ft (100 m) high, which makes it the world's largest flowering plant. The tallest one on record was the 374 ft (114 m) 'Thorpdale' tree in Victoria, which was measured by a surveyor in 1880 just before it was cut down. The tallest hardwood still living today is a mountain ash in Styx

SMALL BUT ANCIENT *Antarctic lichens are small, but may be thousands of years old.*

Valley near Maydena, Tasmania, which measures 322 ft (98 m).

These New World and antipodean giants contrast markedly with plants growing in impoverished or harsh environments such as polar or hot desert regions. The tiny Arctic willow is a species of tree that stands just a few inches tall on the frozen Arctic tundra. At the other end of the world, Antarctic lichens measure barely 4 in (10 cm) in diameter – even though some are probably more than 10 000 years old.

Indeed, some of the oldest inhabitants

of our planet seem to grow in the most inhospitable places. The gnarled, twisted and slow-growing bristlecone pines of the deserts and mountains of Arizona and Nevada are thought to reach ages of 4600 or more years old, while the doughnut-shaped creosote bushes of the Mojave Desert in southern California are 10 000–12 000 years old.

The prize for largest flower goes to the *Rafflesia* of South-east Asia with a diameter of 35 in (90 cm). The plant is parasitic on vines and has thick, fleshy, five-lobed flowers that weigh about 24 lb (11 kg). At the other end of the scale is one of the smallest flowers on Earth: the blossom of *Pilea microphyla*, measuring little more than $1/100$ in (0.25 mm) across. It is widespread in the tropics and known as the artillery or

RECORD LEAF *The giant waterlily of South America has the largest of all leaves.*

pistol plant because of the explosive discharge of pollen from the anthers of the male flowers.

The biggest leaves belong to the giant water lily of tropical South America. The leaves, with upturned edges and a diameter of more than $6^1/2$ feet (2 m), resemble huge pans. They float on the surface of the water and have thick ribs on the underside, making them strong enough to bear the weight of a child.

The broadest crown is held aloft by the banyan tree of India. Numerous prop roots drop from the branches to increase the tree's ability to take up water and minerals and these structures develop into secondary trunks. One specimen, with a crown measuring 1970 ft (600 m) in circumference, was thought to be able to shelter 20 000 people.

The records for greatest girth are held by the African baobab tree and the Mexican swamp cypress. The baobab has a barrel-shaped trunk that may reach 100 ft (30 m) in diameter. It is an adaptation to arid conditions, for the trunk stores water. Some enterprising people have excavated baobabs to make homes. The largest known swamp cypress is *El Gigante* ('The Giant') in the Mexican village of Santa Maria del Tule. The trunk is not round but has huge buttresses, and if the undulations of its outline are followed, the base's circumference is 151 ft (46 m). The great Spanish *conquistador* Hernán Cortés spotted it in the 1520s and described it in his travel diaries. For many years people claimed that *El Gigante* had the thickest trunk of any tree in the world, until it was discovered that its size was the result of three trees having grown and fused together.

LONG LIFE *Some bristlecone pines in the American Rockies may be over 3000 years old.*
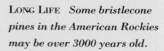

DEFENSIVE TACTICS

Most of the basic foodstuffs needed to sustain life on Earth come from plants. Some plants, however, try to protect themselves from hungry animal predators by being dangerous, poisonous or downright deceptive.

Plants are constantly pestered by browsing animals, but they have evolved effective techniques for fighting them off. Some have thick bark and tough spines to deter large plant-eaters such as deer and antelope. Others mimic inanimate objects such as stones, and are overlooked accordingly. Some recruit allies – ants and wasps, for example – that attack invading herbivorous insects. The most ingenious plants of all protect themselves with unpalatable or even poisonous chemicals. Biological warfare is rife in the natural world.

Leafcutting ants, unlike many other kinds of ant, are a distinct nuisance to plants. They meticulously strip trees of their leaves, and take the pieces back to their nests in order to grow the fungi on which they feed. But one Costa Rican tree, *Hymenaea courbaril*, has made itself safe from leafcutters by producing a fungicide in its leaves. If these leaves were to be transported back to the nest, the chemical would kill the ants' fungus gardens, and the colony would die. The ants therefore avoid the leaves of this tree.

Even simple seaweeds have chemical defences. A brown alga or kelp growing along the Pacific coast of North America produces noxious substances that are based on the caustic white compound phenol, or carbolic acid. These are particularly strong in the fronds supporting its reproductive organs – thus the kelp deters seaweed-eating sea snails from destroying its future generations.

Another class of chemicals used is alkaloids, each of which produces a specific action on particular parts of the nervous system of people and animals. Many plant alkaloids are powerful poisons, such as strychnine from the strychnine tree and coniine in hemlock, which paralyses muscle and nerve endings. Plants are well protected.

THE BAOBAB – GIANT OF THE AFRICAN SAVANNAH

A TREE THAT STORES THOUSANDS OF GALLONS OF WATER FOR SIX MONTHS

Few West African villages are complete without a spreading baobab tree growing on the outskirts, providing welcome midday shade for beasts and humans. One of the largest trees growing in Africa's open savannah lands, the baobab is technically named *Adansonia digitata*, after a French botanist Michel Adanson who travelled in Senegal in the 18th century. The common name 'baobab' is believed to come from the Arabic *bu hibab*, 'fruit of many seeds'.

Its ability to store large amounts of water is one of the baobab's tactics for survival. Although its trunk may reach over 29 ft (9 m) in diameter, it is relatively short, growing to a maximum of 59 ft (18 m).

COLOSSAL PILLARS *A stand of baobab trees rises from a West African lakeside.*

Crooked outspread branches, providing the midday shade, emphasise its squat appearance.

During the rainy season, it stores up to 22 000 gallons (100 000 litres) of water in its soft white fibrous wood to sustain it through the six months of summer. Like many other plants in the region, it then sheds its leaves to limit evaporation from exposed surfaces. When the rains return, the tree grows large white flowers before the leaves appear. The flowers open at night.

The baobab has many uses. The pulp of its gourd-like fruit – also called monkey bread – is rich in vitamin C, and the leaves can be eaten as a vegetable. The baobab's bark can also be pounded into fibres to make rope.

A TWOFOLD ROOTING SYSTEM

Roots play a key role in providing plants with water, and tend to be more developed where the supply is scarce. Plants such as carrots and dandelions sink a basic tap root that may be shallow in temperate regions, but in drier conditions goes much deeper to reach the water table.

Other plants, such as cacluses, live in deserts where rain is rare and underground water hard to reach or non-existent. They are equipped with far-reaching but shallow root systems that enable them to collect moisture from as large an area as possible. They are adapted to conditions in which water may fall in brief, heavy showers, spreading across the surface before soaking into the ground or evaporating. The roots can also absorb some of the dew that condenses overnight.

The African apple-ring thorn-tree – *Acacia albida* – makes use of both survival systems. Its surface roots spread out as far as 40 ft (12 m) from the main plant, while its tap root descends to the water table. This enables it to reverse the seasons: it puts out leaves in the dry season and sheds them when the rain returns.

JUMBO SIZE *An elephant reveals the scale of* Acacia albida's *root system.*

FLOWERS THAT BLOSSOM ON MOUNTAIN SLOPES

GLACIER CROWFOOT AND ALPINE SNOWBELL FLOURISH IN THE SNOW

When rains fall, the barest desert may blossom overnight as plants race to sow their seeds before the drought returns – a condition that may last for years. In the

HARDY GRACE *Glacier crowfoot (below) and the Alpine snowbell (below right) flower above the snowline.*

world's deserts – both cold and hot – plants are dependent on erratic rainfall levels, and must hurry through their life cycles when they have the chance.

In high mountain regions, 'chionophile' (snow-loving) plants have lifestyles adapted to terrain that is permanently cloaked in snow. Unlike varieties from lower altitudes whose life cycle is dictated by the onset of the thaw, chionophile plants develop in the dark, snug beneath blankets of snow.

In the Alps, one example is the glacier crowfoot, *Ranunculus glacialis.* Even at heights of over 9800 ft (3000 m) above sea level, the soil

is rarely frozen beneath 3 to 6 ft (1 to 2 m) of snow. Lightly compacted snow also leaves air pockets that function like small igloos. Here the *Ranunculus* is isolated from the worst of the cold, and is ready to flower as soon as the upper layers of snow begin to melt and let through sunlight. At such high altitudes, the sunlight is particularly rich in ultraviolet radiation, and flowering can start while the outside temperature is still freezing. The glacier

THE PLANT THAT PRETENDS TO BE A STONE

LITHOPS AUCAMPAE

LITHOPS AND REAL STONES

LITHOPS OLIVACEA

In the deserts of southern Africa, pebble plants – also known as 'living stones' – blend so perfectly with their stony background that they can be spotted only during their brief flowering season. It is their way of coping with the threat of passing browsers.

Pebble plants – belonging to the genus *Lithops* – are wily survivors. They are so skilled as mimics that each species is tied to a particular rock formation, imitating its form, colour or texture. Some even reproduce the shine of quartz grains.

At the same time, to tolerate arid climates most *Lithops* have also slimmed down to a single pair of fleshy leaves fused together and often forming a sphere. This is the most effective way of presenting a small surface area to the Sun, while retaining a relatively large volume. Inside their tissues, large cells that are rich in sugar and water are able to survive droughts for weeks on end – indeed, leaves will retain their moisture that long even when snapped off from the main plant.

Every year, new leaves develop in between the two previous ones and absorb their moisture. The old leaves shrivel and die, leaving only scars beneath the new leaves at the base of the plant, which is sunk in the ground. By counting these scars, it is possible to work out a plant's age – some are more than 200 years old.

Another pebble plant, *Fenestraria*, lives buried in sand except for a window of crystals that protrudes above the ground and concentrates the sunlight it receives.

crowfoot has been found in Switzerland at heights of 14 000 ft (4275m), a record for flowering plants in Europe.

Another similar chionophile plant is the Alpine snowbell, *Soldanella alpina*. To speed up seed production, the mauve or white flowers often appear before the leaves, as the snow is thawing.

ACACIAS AND ANTS – A FIGHTING PARTNERSHIP

ANTS REPEL ANIMAL INTRUDERS
IN RETURN FOR FOOD AND SHELTER

An alliance with ants is the secret of the Central American plant *Acacia cornigera* – the name means 'horn-bearer'. Its 'horns' are large thorns – a powerful deterrent in themselves, but doubly protective because their hollow interiors offer shelter to *Pseudomyrex* ants. Access for the ants is easy, through a softer, less woody section at the base of each thorn. Once inside, they find a natural nest, already provided with two handy compartments: one for adults, one for their young.

The acacia's leaf stalks even bear glands whose nectar feeds the ants. This special 'baby food' is produced at the tips of the young leaves, and harvested when they mature.

The ants repay the acacia's hospitality by attacking animal intruders. They also protect their hosts from other plants by biting off

ANT FRIENDS *Ants find a home with* Acacia cornigera.

KILLER SAP *The milkweed's poisonous sap kills most insects.*

any vine shoots or tree branches that look as if they might interfere with their growth. The relationship is so successful that if the tree loses its ants it may find itself choked by invading vegetation.

Similarly, on the Malay peninsula there are species of stingless ant that protect *Macaranga* trees in the spurge family. A young tree must compete with other plants, particularly vines, at the edge of the forest where there is competition for space and light. The ants nest in hollows in the stem of the *Macaranga* tree, and pay it back by clearing away competing plants. They also clear lichens and fungi from its leaf surfaces and remove the eggs of herbivorous insects.

POISON AS A PROTECTION FROM PREDATORS

POISONS AND DECEPTIVE FRAGRANCES PUNISH HERBIVORES TO THEIR DEATH

One extremely effective defence for plants is poison. *Asclepias curassavica,* for example, is a member of the milkweed family found in tropical America and contains a poison lethal to insects in its latex – a milky rubbery liquid that oozes profusely when the leaves or stems are damaged.

It also yields a fragrant nectar that is not toxic but scarcely less dangerous. When

FLY REPELLENT *The tansy's aromatic leaves are unpleasant to insects.*

bees are lured by the fragrance to pollinate the plant, some pay with their lives, caught in a trapdoor system that only the strongest can escape, though not before they drop their pollen sacs. The rest will die in the trap. Other species of milkweed produce poison that can damage and even kill much larger animals, including sheep.

The tansy, *Tanacetum vulgare,* contains chemicals less dangerous than the milkweed's, but with a strong smell that repels insects. It shares this property with various species of the Compositae family, which includes daisies, marigolds and dandelions. One of these, *Tanacetum cinerariifolium* which grows in western Asia, provides a very effective insecticide powder.

However, it is possible for adaptation to protect aggressors against these plant poisons. The American monarch butterfly, *Danaus plexippus,* for instance, has become so immune to the substances contained in *Asclepias,* that it lays its eggs on the plant. It even stockpiles the poison internally to make itself toxic to predators.

Having been thwarted by insects such as the monarch butterfly caterpillar, plants have taken to other defensive strategies: they mimic the hormones and pheromones (substances secreted by some animals to produce responses in others of the same species) that regulate insect lives. Insects react to these substances automatically,

and being able to produce them gives a plant the upper hand. Wild potato plants have taken up the challenge and produce the alarm pheromones of potato aphids. It sends the aphids packing. Other chemicals

WATER COLLECTORS

In the sultanate of Oman in the Middle East, a cistern dug at the foot of an olive tree and a rhamnus – a buckthorn plant – collects up to 40 gallons (180 litres) of fresh water every day. In the Canary Islands, visitors can still see six open-air wells that used to fill with water condensed by a tree that no longer grows there: it was a kind of stinkwood, *Ocotea foetens.*

In several dry mountain regions scattered around the world, there are plants that have adapted in this way to become hidden springs, often used by people as well as the plant itself. Hairs on the rough upper surfaces of their leaves capture water vapour from mists and the merest drizzle of rain, which then condenses to trickle down the plant.

This characteristic enables many plants to survive outside their usual climate zones. The beeches on the sea coast of the Saint-Beaume massif, near Marseille, for example, live in a climate that ought to be much too dry for them. But sea air rising up the steep incline of the massif creates the mists that keep them alive.

produced by plants such as ferns prevent insects from moulting and thus growing.

Another option is for a plant to produce substances that reduce the nutritive value of its leaves. By reducing the amount of tannins in leaves they can make them

THE PASSIONFLOWER: SIEGE WARFARE

There are nearly 500 species of passionflower, and most have devised ways to discourage the 500 species of *Heliconius* butterfly that strive to rear larvae on their foliage.

In the course of evolution, the butterflies have focused on the point when the young leaves are just large enough to make room for their eggs. When the caterpillars hatch, they attack the leaves and weaken the plant. Some passionflowers have attempted to alter the look of their leaves during the egg-laying season, but *Heliconius* has countered this visual tactic: it is able to identify the flowers by their chemical characteristics.

Undaunted, some species of passionflower have developed a nectar gland that lures stinging ants to fight off predators. Others have grown poisonous spines that can impale a caterpillar. Others have cells that grow into blobs that look like a batch of eggs. The female butterfly, sensing competition, abandons the plant and lays her eggs elsewhere.

E arly Spanish settlers in the American tropics saw the passionflower as an emblem of Christ's Crucifixion (or Passion): its corona stood for the Crown of Thorns, the styles for the nails on the Cross, and so on. To naturalists,

CRUCIFIED *A passionflower reveals the nails – its stamens – and the crown of thorns.*

the most striking feature of the passionflower – a kind of vine – is its endless battle with butterflies.

HELICONIUS BUTTERFLY

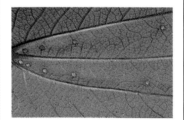

FALSE 'EGGS' ON THE LEAVES

---

more difficult to digest. Bracken is a plant which draws on an arsenal of these chemical weapons, including cyanide, thiaminase, tannin and silicate. As the summer progresses, however, and the plant weakens, the defences decrease and the number of herbivores on its leaves increases.

THE PAINFUL PRICE OF TEMPTATION

SUCCULENT PLANTS DEVISE RUTHLESS

STRATEGIES FOR SURVIVAL

Most members of the Araceae family – which includes arum lilies and the 'fruit salad' vine – are succulent and tempting to herbivores, so they have had to develop ways of surviving. Some grow high up on trees, and thus out of the reach of many predators; others, such as the taro or eddo, *Colocasia esculenta*, keep their big starchy tubers – a staple in the diet of many Pacific islanders – underground.

Members of the family that grow at ground level have been compelled to develop more elaborate defences. These include various species of *Dieffenbachia*, or 'dumb-cane' – originally a tropical plant. Exposed among damp undergrowth or on riverbanks, their plump stems make them too appetising for a hungry passer-by to ignore, and natural selection has favoured those that can create toxic substances. *Dieffenbachia seguine* produces sap that turns viscous when the stem is broken. It contains oxalic acid (also used as a laundry bleach), and causes painful inflammations of the mucous membranes in the nose

SKUNK CABBAGE *The purple-hued* Symplocarpus foetidus *warns off would-be predators with a foul smell.*

POISON BEAUTY *Its flowers and leaves look tasty, but* Lysichitum Americanum *has toxic defences of oxalic acid.*

and mouth. In India, it was once used to torture slaves, who were forced to swallow a piece, which turned them temporarily mute. The same poison occurs in *Symplocarpus foetidus*, which smells as unpleasant as its Latin name suggests, and goes by the common name of 'skunk cabbage'.

Poisonous alkaloids causing paralysis or even death are potent defences against animals or humans. The strychnine tree (*Strychnos nuxvomica*) in India and the vine known as Saint Ignatius' beans (*Strychnos ignatii*) in the Philippines are both members of the genus *Strychnos*, producing, as their name suggests, the poison strychnine,

often used against rats. Other plant alkaloids, however, can be put to good use, including codeine, morphine and quinine, all of which have pharmaceutical value.

DEFENCE TACTICS IN DELAYED-ACTION BOMBS

STERILITY AND MALFORMATION TAKE LONG-TERM TOLL ON RASH PREDATORS

Thorns, toxic substances, nauseating smells – all are instant deterrents. And for the most part, they are effective, even if some stubborn browsers die when the warning signals fail. Some plants, however, use less short-term methods, and practise forms of biological warfare that may exterminate or reduce entire populations.

Ageratum houstonianum, a small ornamental plant with blue flowers, does nothing to warn off insects that attack it, but strikes back against future generations. When the insects eat it, they absorb a chemical that acts on the juvenile hormone and causes the larvae to develop prematurely into sterile adults.

Azadirachta indica, the Indian lilac, a member of the mahogany family (Meliaceae),

DELAYED-ACTION KILLER *Ageratum secretes a chemical that sterilises the larvae of insects feeding on it.*

The stinging nettle, *Urtica dioica,* was once used to make beer. It is still used to make tea and can be boiled as a vegetable, not unlike spinach in taste and texture. But touch it carelessly and it can be uncomfortably painful – unless you grasp it firmly with the fingers where the skin is tougher.

It protects itself from foragers with hollow hairs containing formic acid and histamines. When an animal or person touches a nettle, the tips of the hairs break off to leave jagged tips – like deadly hypodermics. These scratch the surface of the skin and inject the painful fluid.

Some browsing animals with tender mouths and nostrils are rebuffed, but a lot of cattle have developed an immunity to stinging nettles.

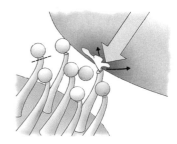

SYRINGES *Nettle hairs inject painful fluid.*

has fruits that are rich in azadirachtine, a compound causing genetic damage. The larvae of insects consuming it suffer a higher than normal mortality rate or skip certain larval stages to become smaller, sickly adults, sometimes unable to breed.

Insects are not the only targets. Some plants make compounds that mimic the function of the steroid hormone oestrogen in mammals and lower the fertility of animals consuming them.

TRIUMPHS OF REPRODUCTION

Inbreeding can lead to weakness among plants, as well as among animals and humans. Nature has found many ingenious ways of ensuring healthy reproduction in the plant kingdom, and of distributing the seeds that result.

Sex is as vital to the 300 000 known species of plants as it is to animals. Plants, like any other living things, must be strong to survive, and so, to avoid inbreeding, they must swap genes with unrelated members of the same species. In this way, they keep the stock healthy and able to resist disease.

But while most animals are able to move about easily, enabling males to find and court unrelated females and then to procreate, most plants have a fundamental disadvantage: they are rooted to the spot. So they enlist the help of animals, such as insects, birds and bats, and the elements, such as wind and water, to convey pollen – which plays the 'male' role in plant fertilisation – from one flower to another.

The adaptations that have resulted, particularly those involving animals, are often bizarre, but at the same time they are always effective. During

DECEPTION *Both fly orchids (right) and bee orchids (below) mimic the smell and shape of the female insects.*

the course of evolution, the lives of the two protagonists – plants and animals – have somehow become so tangled up with one another that neither can survive without the other. Honeysuckles, for example, store their nectar so far down in the flower's narrow tube that only hawk moths, with their very long proboscis, can reach the sweet liquid. The plant makes sure to attract the appropriate guest by producing the right fragrance at night when moths are

about. The long-tongued, night-flying hawk moth is, therefore, one of the few insects that will bother to visit honeysuckle. It receives a dusting of pollen, which it carries to its next floral rendezvous, and gains a reward of nectar for its trouble. Both benefit: the moth gets a meal and the plant is pollinated – an arrangement that primitive plants and insects are thought to have started about 125 million years ago.

And after the inevitable fertilisation has taken place, there are equally ingenious means to distribute the seeds or, in the case of different but no less cleverly engineered life forms such as fungi, to disperse the spores.

POLLINATED BY SEXUAL DECEPTION

ORCHIDS DUPE WASPS AND BEES BY IMITATING THE LURE OF FEMALES

Orchids originating in the Mediterranean region use sexual deception to lure bees and wasps into pollinating their flowers. They are *Ophrys* orchids, a genus of some 30 different species, with metallic-coloured flowers and including the European bee and fly orchids.

To achieve their ends, *Ophrys* orchids first attract male bees and wasps by imitating the smell secreted by the abdominal glands of the female insects. Then, to make doubly sure, the orchids' labellum – the upper petal of the corolla – closely mimics the shape and colours of the female. Like the female's abdomen, it even has a furry texture. This last feature particularly excites the male when he has

landed on the flower, while the scent stimulus ensures that he stays long enough for the orchid to pack two small pollen sacs on his back. These are subsequently deposited on the pistil (female reproductive organ) of the next flower he finds himself seduced into visiting.

Some orchids offer no obvious reward in the shape of food, yet they still enlist the help of insects to carry pollen from flower to flower. Flowers of *Serapias*, for example,

found in low-lying damp areas in the Middle East, provide refuge for solitary bees. The female bees normally spend the night in holes in the ground, and males enter the holes in search of the females. The orchid's flower mimics a bee's nighttime haven, complete with a long tube and an enticing hole.

As the insect enters, however, its passage is partially blocked by the orchid's collection of sexual parts, known as the

PURPLE SHADES *Some* Ophrys *orchids – such as the mirror orchid (above) – imitate female insects' furry bodies.*

column. While attempting to force its way through this, the bee is daubed with pollen. Unsuccessful in its first attempts to enter, it flies to another 'hole' and pollination is achieved. Towards the evening, the orchid relents and the bee is able to push its way past the column and

HIJACKED *A bee falls into the bucket orchid's trap. Then, as it forces its way out, it cannot help collecting a coat of pollen grains, which it will carry to other flowers.*

SCENTED JAIL *Bucket orchids trap and drug prospecting bees.*

into the flower, where it spends the night. In the morning, the heat of the Sun warms both flower and bee and the daily routine begins all over again.

ORCHIDS THAT KIDNAP BEES WITH NARCOTICS

FRAGRANT INTOXICANTS DRUG BEES
LONG ENOUGH FOR POLLINATION

The orchid *Coryanthes speciosa* from the rain-forests of Central and South America has developed a rather devious pollination system. When its large flowers reach maturity, they fold back their petals and sepals to reveal an oddly shaped labellum whose bulging lower half becomes a small bowl filled with liquid siphoned into it by the orchid itself.

When the flowers are open, the base of the labellum gives off a powerful scent that attracts male bees. These fragrant compounds also have an intoxicating effect, so that the doped visitor loses his footing and topples into the liquid. The only way out of the trap is a narrow tunnel lined with pollen. He emerges carrying clusters of pollen to be deposited on the pistil of the next flower he visits. However, it is not always a simple process: sometimes it can take an insect 45 minutes to find its way out.

The host does not release its fragrance again until the following morning and,

since the same bee is unlikely to make two consecutive visits, this protects the orchid from self-fertilisation.

Although botanists have identified a dozen *Coryanthes* species, often living as neighbours, all are epiphytic – plants that live on other plants but are not parasitic. It seems that the orchids give off different smells, luring different insects, and so preserve their species from interbreeding.

THE BOTANICAL IMPRESSIONISTS

FLOWERS THAT FAKE CARRION TO
ATTRACT FLIES AND SPREAD SPORES

Leafless *Stapelias* are small succulent plants that can go unnoticed on the plains of tropical and southern Africa . . . except when they bloom. When that happens, they

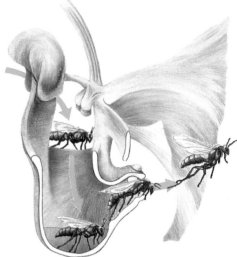

are hard to miss. The brownish or reddish flowers are thick and fleshy, and in the case of *Stapelia gigantea* may measure as much as 18 in (46 cm) across.

As well as looking rather like a piece of rotting meat, they also have a similar smell – not as a deterrent to herbivores, but as a lure for pollinators. Saprophagous flies – flies that live on decomposing matter – are

FAKE-FLESH FLOWERS *Flies mistake* Stapelia gigantea *(below) for rotten meat. The huge flowers of* Rafflesia *(right) even smell like rotting flesh.*

deceived by the *Stapelia*'s fake carrion into landing on the flower to lay eggs. Their legs collect pollen, and thus they help to fertilise the next flower they visit.

Stapelia is not the only plant to give off smells of rotting flesh in order to propagate itself. Stinkhorn fungi produce obnoxious liquids that make whole woodlands smell of putrefaction in order to attract the flies that spread their spores. The parasitic plant *Rafflesia* lives on the roots of liana vines in tropical South-east Asia. It has developed the same strategy as *Stapelia*, mimicking both the smell and appearance of a carcass on the forest floor, except that *Rafflesia*'s giant flowers are much larger than *Stapelia*'s. They grow up to 36 in (91 cm) across – larger than any other flower.

THE SCENT OF DANGER

ARISTOLOCHIA LURES INSECTS

INTO A FRAGRANT PRISON

An S-shaped tube that flares at the end like the bell of a French horn serves as a flower for the 500 species of shrubs and herbs belonging to the genus *Aristolochia*. Instead of petals, the plants – which include wild ginger and different kinds of birthwort – have a colourful calyx (a flower's protective outer covering, usually consisting of green, leaflike sepals). This is fused at its lip into a tube that provides a tempting landing zone for pollinators.

Some of these species have ways of arresting and detaining visiting insects until they have paid their pollinating dues. One method is to smell so attractive that the insect ventures deep into the broad bell of the tube until it sets foot on a slippery surface and slithers to the bottom. There, light filtering through translucent areas located near the stamens guides it along a narrow tunnel to the end of the tube. The insect remains imprisoned until the stamens ripen, which may take several hours, and its body is covered with pollen.

LURED IN *Aristolochia grandis (top) and A. rotunda (above) lure insects into their flowers. The stamen chambers (right) act as prisons for them.*

Way in
An attractive smell lures the insect down the tube into the stamen 'chamber'.

Way out
After the stamens have ripened, the tunnel expands and the insect is released.

THE FIG'S THREE-STAGE STRUGGLE FOR SURVIVAL

As meat is to carnivores, so figs are to fruit-eating creatures. In tropical rain forests all over the world, no source of food matters more than the many species of wild fig, from the slender individual trees to the massively buttressed strangler figs and the giant multi-pillared banyan trees bearing hundreds of pounds of fruit. Dozens of different species of birds and mammals may feed on a single tree. If figs had fewer methods of pollinating there might be times when their food was no longer available – a loss that would massively reduce the animal populations of the tropics. As it is, this staple food of the rain forest is produced by a multiple back-up system that uses as many different pollinators as there are species to pollinate.

The flowers of the fig tree are enclosed inside a succulent receptacle with only a single tiny entrance, the ostiole, that leads to the outside. When it reaches maturity, this receptacle swells to become the developed 'fruit' (in technical terms an infructescence) – in fact, consisting of thousands of tiny fruits embedded in the edible flesh of the receptacle.

There are 800 different species of fig, and the pollination of each one is among the most complex and exacting of all interactions between a plant and its pollinators. It is a relationship that has evolved throughout the tropical and subtropical world, as well as in temperate regions. Each species is not only pollinated but also inhabited by its own species of

wasp. In the case of *Ficus carica*, the common fig from which the familiar cultivated fig was developed, the insect is the wasp, *Blastophaga grossorum*.

Ficus carica bears three types of figs in succession. The spring variety is not succulent. It has male, pollen-making flowers near the ostiole, with female but sterile flowers called 'gall flowers' provided for the use of the pollinator wasps. Summer figs are full of gall flowers, as well as the fertile female flowers that produce the seeds in the figs we eat. Last come the autumn figs, which remain on the

FAST FOOD *Many animals eat the common fig's lush red flesh and spread its seeds.*

tree and contain nothing but gall flowers.

These three types of fig are linked with three different generations of the *Blastophaga* wasp. The females of the first generation enter the spring figs by way of the ostiole. They lay their eggs in the gall flowers, and then die. The eggs mature inside the fig and create the second generation of wasps, both male and female. The wingless males fertilise the females, then die. The females load themselves up with pollen, leave through the ostiole, and fly off to the summer, female-phase figs, where they fertilise the fig and lay their own eggs in the gall flowers. The third generation is on its way. As in springtime, only the fertilised females will emerge when autumn begins.

The females now proceed to the autumn figs and lay their eggs in the gall flowers. The young wasps hatch before winter comes, but remain inside their quarters, only the females emerging in the spring. This pattern is echoed, with variations, in other fig-tree species equally dependent upon other partner wasps.

WASP AID *A live-in wasp pollinates the common fig.*

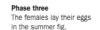

Phase two
Winged and fertilised females leave the fig.

Phase one
Blastophaga wasp eggs mature inside the spring fig.

Phase three
The females lay their eggs in the summer fig.

Female flyers
The wingless males die after they have fertilised the females.

Inside flowers
The female, male and sterile 'gall' flowers are contained inside the fig.

Only then does the tunnel expand to release the trapped creature.

Other species detain insects that reach the end of the calyx by lining the tube with downward-pointing hairs that act as valves in a one-way system. Others generate high temperatures so welcome to the pollinator that it stays of its own accord.

DEADLY HOSTS

WATER-LILY FLOWERS SNAP SHUT OVER STRAY INSECTS

Many water lilies have a habit of opening their flowers to admit pollinators – which range from large beetles to much smaller insects – and then closing to detain their visitors. A prisoner will thrash about among the stamens for 24 hours, and is not released until it is covered with pollen. The same thing happens when it visits the next water-lily flower, when it has to spend another day unloading its pollen cargo.

In South Africa, the Cape water lily (*Nymphaea capensis*) is fatal to its pollinators. For two or three days – while the stamens (male organs) are still immature – its flowers are female. Various species of

FLOWERY EMBRACE *Water lilies fold their petals around visiting insects, and detain them until covered in pollen.*

WATER BOMBS *The pressurised fruit of* Ecballium elaterium *burst open if touched, and thus spread their seeds.*

small *Syrphus* flies visit it and fall into a pool of liquid inside the flower. In their struggle to escape they release the pollen on their bodies, which sinks to the bottom of the pool where it fertilises the female organs. At nightfall the flower closes and imprisons the fly in what becomes its tomb. Eventually the stamens mature and visiting flies are no longer in danger of drowning – they fly off with their cargo of pollen, but soon fall victims to the next female flower they visit.

Water lilies cannot live outside their watery habitat, even though they have to flower and be pollinated in the open air. The flowers develop underwater on a stalk known as a 'pedicel', which then grows up to the surface to allow the bud to bloom. The fruit reverses this procedure: when it is shed, it falls to the bottom and there it decays, releasing buoyant

seeds that float back to the surface. Some of these seeds then cling to the feathers of water birds and are airlifted to populate other waters.

EXPLOSIVE EJECTORS

SEEDS TOO HEAVY FOR THE WIND ARE CATAPULTED AWAY LIKE MISSILES

Some seeds are too heavy to float or glide, yet the parent plant still has to ensure its survival. One solution is forcible expulsion by means of a catapult, blowpipe or grenade. The extremely ingenious mechanisms that trigger ejection are often linked to severe droughts, heavy rains or sharp changes in atmospheric humidity. They exploit the resulting differences in pressure between one part of the plant and another.

The balsam family carries hard black seeds in a drop-shaped capsule that is enclosed by an outer skin consisting of several jointed sections or valves. These are seamed like the strips of a leather ball, and at seeding time they are blown up very tight by the liquids inside them, their cells stretching like elastic. At this stage, the slightest touch overloads the tension; the valves spring together from the ends with an audible crack, and the seeds explode through the gaping seams to scatter over a radius of several yards.

As it ripens, the succulent yellow fruit of the Mediterranean *Ecballium elaterium* fills with water. When mature, the cells are so swollen that they compress the seeds and internal liquid. You have only to brush against the fruit for it to detach itself from the plant and squirt pressurised jets of seeds and liquid up to 39 ft (12 m).

THE FUNGUS THAT HUNTS WITH A HARPOON

HUNTER FUNGI FIRE SPORES INTO TINY WORMS BEFORE REPRODUCING

The hunter fungus is armed with a kind of pointed harpoon that it uses to fire a payload of its own spores into the tissues of tiny worms known as nematodes. The spores put out mycelia, networks of threads that colonise the body of the worm and feed on it before they reproduce. They then release more 'harpoonist' cells to await the next live target. Nematode worms are well able to withstand their hunters' inroads. A single female nematode can lay 200 000 eggs a day, and one authority records that the top $^3/_4$ in (2 cm) of an acre (0.4 ha) of rich soil contains about a billion individuals.

REPRODUCTIVE BALLISTICS

BIRD'S-NEST FUNGUS LAUNCHES SPORES ON A FAR TRAJECTORY

A tiny variety of bird's-nest fungus, measuring no more than $^1/_5$ in (5 mm) across, probably holds a world record for throwing. *Sphaerobolus stellatus*, the starred spherethrower, grows on rotting plant matter.

It starts out shaped like a globe, and then opens into a yellowish-orange starshaped cup, displaying a cream-coloured body shaped like an egg inside it. This is called the peridiole, and soon turns brownish and viscous. At maturity, and when the

NEST EGGS *Bird's nest fungi have 'eggs' that flip out when raindrops hit them.*

weather is right, a membrane lining the cup goes into spasm, flips outwards, and launches the peridiole more than 13 ft (4 m) high and over a distance of up to 18 ft (5.5 m). Proportionately, it is the equivalent of a human being kicking a football well over a mile (1.6 km) high and nearly 2 miles (3.2 km) distant.

Such a burst of energy is produced solely for the sake of reproduction. The peridiole contains spores, and its viscous coating makes sure that it will stick where it lands, unless some herbivore swallows it, in which case it will travel farther still.

SEDUCED BY AN ORCHID

Wingless female wasps ensure the survival of orchids found only in south-west Australia. The genus *Drakaea* includes only four species. They are small, with one heart-shaped leaf and an unusual flower, and they share interlocked lives with a species of wasp whose females live underground. Like some other orchids, *Drakaea* use sexual deception to ensure their survival.

In the mating season, the female emerges from her lair. Because she is unable to fly, she climbs a tree and broadcasts hormones that attract the males. The larger, strong-winged male seizes the female and carries her away for a nuptial flight. *Drakaea*

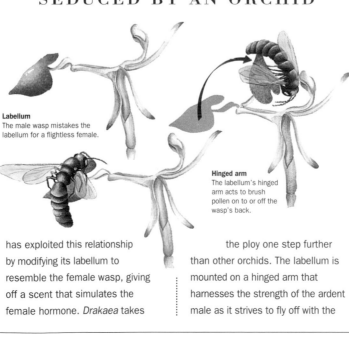

Labellum
The male wasp mistakes the labellum for a flightless female.

Hinged arm
The labellum's hinged arm acts to brush pollen on to or off the wasp's back.

has exploited this relationship by modifying its labellum to resemble the female wasp, giving off a scent that simulates the female hormone. *Drakaea* takes the ploy one step further than other orchids. The labellum is mounted on a hinged arm that harnesses the strength of the ardent male as it strives to fly off with the

FERTILE DECEPTION *A male wasp mistakes the* Drakaea *orchid for a female, and helps pollination.*

phantom female. Acting like a piston, it dashes the male against the fertile part of the flower to coat it with pollen. Eventually the wasp gives up its efforts to elope with an inflexible female and flies off to try again elsewhere. If it meets another *Drakaea* the deception is repeated, and the pollen on its back is forcibly delivered where it can fertilise the flower. With luck, the wasp will eventually happen upon a genuine female of its species.

Travelling Seeds

Plants have to expand to survive, constantly conquering new territory, in order to set up new colonies of the species. For this process, they have developed several sophisticated strategies, not only to fertilise each other, but also to deliver their seeds to sites that favour the germination of each species.

Travelling inside the very animals that feed off them is one such technique. Passing through an animal's stomach does a seed no harm, and has led to a specialised means of transport for the tender seeds of many fleshy fruits. Thrushes, for example, are partial to the fine white berries of the parasitic plant, mistletoe (*Viscum album*). They pay for its tasty pulp by conveying its seeds to the warmth of their stomachs, from where the seeds are later excreted to fall on the bark of a suitable host tree. The Chinese fruit lychees (*Litchi chinensis*) have a juicy pulp under their hard, knobbly skins. This is especially attractive to monkeys, who also spread the seeds to new places.

Some fruits not only wrap their seeds in a tasty coating, but also dress them up in attractive colours. The rich red of cherries, for instance, is an important part of their appeal. The rosary pea (*Abrus precatorius*) goes a step farther. Its seeds are clad in red and black but have no food to offer. Birds are attracted all the same, swallowing the seeds and then carrying them off with them.

SEED BEARERS *Thrushes help to propagate the mistletoe plant. They eat the berries and carry the seeds to new places.*

Rather than pay for their ride, some fruits have adopted a more direct approach. They just hang on to passers-by. Examples are the burrs of the great burdock (*Arctium lappa*), and the hooked bristles of goose grass or cleavers (*Galium aparine*), wild carrot (*Daucus carota*) and shepherd's purse (*Capsella bursa-pastoris*). All these cling to the fleece of sheep or other furry animals and the socks and clothing of human ramblers. It was the massed bristles of agrimony (*Agrimonia eupatoria*) hooking themselves onto fur or clothing that inspired the inventor of Velcro.

These and similar methods of dispersing seeds share a drawback, however:

CLINGING ON TIGHT *Burrs, such as those of the plant agrimony, fasten themselves onto the fur of passing animals or people's clothing.*

they need a living creature to make them work. Another way in which plants are able to scatter their seeds is by exploiting the vagaries of the wind.

The fruits of the elm tree (*Ulmus Ulmus*), the common ash (*Fraxinus excelsior*), the lime (*Tilia*), and the hornbeam (*Carpinus betulus*) are all fitted with aerofoils. These are flat papery-thin membranes veined like a dragonfly's wing, which enable them to glide over remarkably long distances. The seed of the maple (*Acer*) is long and curved like a propeller blade and can fly hundreds of yards when the wind is right. It spins as it falls, and the spin slows it down and takes it even farther.

The most highly developed of all these airborne embryos is unquestionably the seed of *Zanonia*, a climbing plant of the Cucurbitaceae family, whose 6 in (15 cm) wingspan launches it from the top of tall

supporting trees. The Austrian, Igo Etrich, based one of his early gliders on its design in 1922.

Other families of plants, such as the Asclepidaceae (the milkweed family) and the numerous Compositae or Asteraceae, have members that specialise in floating through the air rather than gliding, with the help of downs and bristles that catch the lightest of breezes. The seeds of the dandelion (*Taraxacum officinale*), for example, can drift for several miles. If they land in water, their parachutes convert into small boats, with their bristles curling back to raise them above the surface of the water like a sail. Sometimes, bristles like these are spun into silky hairs, as in cotton grass (*Eriophorum*) or cotton itself (*Gossypium*).

Often, the simplest technique can be the most effective. Conifers rely on massproduction and the wind to broadcast billions of pollen grains and to saturate their environment in a random quest for female seed cones. In the same way, orchids have specialised in producing tiny seeds. Barely larger than pollen dust, they are light enough to drift wherever air currents travel. Because of their microscopic size,

SATURATION *Catkins release huge clouds of pollen grains. Some of the grains will pollinate another plant.*

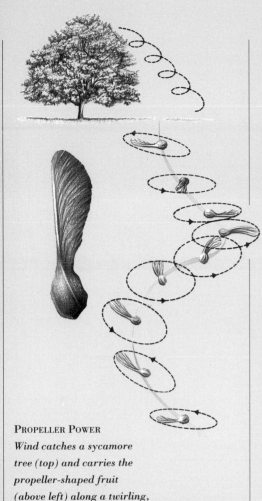

PROPELLER POWER

Wind catches a sycamore tree (top) and carries the propeller-shaped fruit (above left) along a twirling, zigzag path (above right).

LIFT OFF *Puffs of wind blow the dandelion's downy parachutes.*

they can be produced in tremendous quantities: a single capsule of one *Maxillaria* orchid holds a colossal 100 000 seeds or more.

Aquatic plants, meanwhile, exploit the water to disperse their seeds throughout their habitat. The *Nelumbo* genus of water lilies, which includes the oriental sacred lotus, keeps its seeds in a receptacle shaped like the rose of a watering can. When it is ripe, the receptacle breaks loose from the plant and drifts away. Eventually it rots; the seeds are released and sink into the mud to germinate. The seed capsule of the white water lily, *Nymphaea alba*, ripens under water. At maturity, it splits open and releases seeds whose coats contain air bubbles and which swell up on contact with the water. The seeds float off on the water currents until they, too, sink to the bottom and sprout.

The long-distance champion of all aquatic seeds is the coconut palm, *Cocos nucifera*, symbol of tropical delights and flourishing along sea coasts throughout the tropical regions of the world. The palm wraps its large buoyant fruits in a thick fibrous coat. As a result, a coconut that drops into the sea might be afloat for months before it is washed ashore again; even so, it will still take root. The travels of the coconut palm have been so hard to trace that botanists are not yet agreed on its country of origin.

Some plants play safe and adopt more than one method of dispersal. Thus, the seeds of gorse *Ulex* are violently ejected when the pod splits, scattering them far and wide. At the same time, an oily outgrowth on the seed, known as a 'caruncle' or 'elaiosome', makes them attractive to ants which carry them away. Indeed, ants are a favourite method of seed dispersal: over 3000 species of flowering plants, found on every continent except Antarctica, rely on these busy little insects. Examples include the wild flower *Trillium petiolatum* from North America and the violet of Europe, which grow close to the ground to make it easier for ants to reach the seeds. The seeds bear elaiosomes to attract the ants. The ants eat the fat and leave the seeds which later germinate.

OCEAN ROVER *Coconuts are carried thousands of miles by sea.*

OUTLAWS AND ODD ONES OUT

Strangling, trapping, drowning and smothering – the techniques are brutal, and the perpetrators are unexpected. The killers are in fact plants, from fig trees to flesh-eating pitcher plants, determined to ensure their own survival.

Certain kinds of plants get back at vexatious animals – by eating them. Most plants survive on a diet of sun, water, carbon dioxide and minerals from the soil. Some, however, supplement all this with meat, which has the advantage that it enables them to survive in poor conditions.

Carnivorous plants are mostly found in damp places where the soil is acid, boggy and peaty, and where there is a deficiency in essential plant foods, such as those containing nitrogen. They make good these nutritional shortcomings by catching and digesting insects, as well as some other small animals, and absorbing nitrogen-rich fluid from them. Digestion is so efficient that only the hard wing-cases and outer skeletons of insects remain intact.

The traps and snares are ingenious, ranging in complexity from the simple, roughly trumpet-shaped tube of the pitcher plant, through sticky sundews, to the sophisticated Venus flytrap with its hair-like trigger and formidable jaws. There are 'passive' traps, which are rather like simple pitfalls, and there are 'active' snares, which capture creatures with mechanisms, rather like mousetraps. There are even plants that act like moving flypapers, using cunning contrivances modified from leaves or tendrils.

But these flesh-eaters are not the only predators of the plant world: even more astonishing in many ways is the fig, which gradually wraps itself around an unsuspecting host plant, and then squeezes tight and chokes it to death.

THE CARNIVOROUS PLANT THAT DROWNS ITS VICTIMS

PITCHER PLANTS FEED ON CREATURES FROM ANTS TO RATS

Meat-eating animals that stalk their prey generally aim to be as quiet and unobtrusive as possible. The opposite is true of the carnivorous pitcher plant, *Nepenthes*, whose 70-odd species inhabit the tropical rain forests of Madagascar, Asia and Australia.

They have developed a distinctive and specialised organ that grows on tendrils extending from the tips of their leaves.

AERIAL GRACE *Despite their beauty, Nepenthes rafflesiana (left) and N. villosa (right) are deadly meat-eaters. Previous pages: Clusters of ground-dwelling pitcher plants gape at the sky.*

The dangling tendril swells at the end, curves upwards and then inflates into a 'pitcher', often capped by a colourful lid. Its mouth folds downwards and outwards to form a rim that acts as a platform for insects lured by nectar glands around the lid and mouth. The foothold for insects is treacherous and borders on an area covered with a crumbly wax. Once an insect begins to slip, it slithers helplessly to the bottom of the pitcher, which is filled with a nauseous liquid. Then the digestive glands begin to pump acids and enzymes into the drowning pool to start digesting its victim.

Some *Nepenthes* species have miniature pitchers no more than 2 in (5 cm) long. The largest and the most formidable, however, is *Nepenthes rafflesiana*. It can be up to 30 ft (9 m) tall, with pitchers 3-12 in (8-30 cm) wide. As well as ants and flying insects, large beetles, centipedes, scorpions and sometimes even reptiles have fallen captive to its lure.

THE DEADLY THREAT OF A STICKY END

ON THE SUNDEW, ALL THAT GLITTERS IS NOT NECTAR

Insects visiting the sundew, *Drosera*, are doomed to a sticky end. *Drosera* is found on boggy, acid soils all over the world from the Arctic to tropical regions. It usually appears as a small, jewel-like plant that glistens in sunlight, with leaves growing in rosettes a few inches across.

The leaves may be roundish, spoon-shaped, or so long and narrow that they look more like stems. The upper surface of the leaf-blades teems with short pink or reddish tentacles, swelling at the end into an oval gland bearing a drop of clear sticky fluid. No matter which way the tentacle is pointing, the globe

RED DEATH *Each tentacle of the common sundew (inset) carries a fluid that can hold and digest its prey – such as a lacewing fly (main picture).*

hardly changes its shape. As the whole plant is covered with thousands of these orbs, the Sun can dress it in a coat of light.

The orbs are apparently odourless, yet look like nectar glistening in the flower and so attract insects. However, landing on its leaves is likely to prove a creature's final act: as soon as it brushes against a single viscous orb, it sticks fast, and the more it struggles, the more nearby tentacles cling on to it. The tentacles are longer at the edge of the leaf, and have a reflex that makes them bend inwards at the touch of a prey, forcing victims towards the middle.

The sundew's glands are in effect multi-purpose factories. They manufacture the sticky mucus that captures the visiting insect; they secrete the acid and enzymes that liquidise the victim, and they help to absorb the edible broth it provides.

AIR NODULES *The air-filled bags – or bladders – give the greater bladderwort its name.*

VICIOUS SUCTION TRAPS

SUBMARINE RECEPTACLES

SWALLOW VICTIMS FOR FOOD

The greater bladderwort, *Utricularia vulgaris*, is equipped with wildlife traps as cunningly designed as the bladders that give the plant its name. Entirely submerged except when it flowers, it appears as a mass of underwater stems and shoots growing up to 9 ft (2.75 m) long. It has no roots, and with narrow stem-like leaves, looks more like algae than a flowering plant.

Utricularia vulgaris lives in ponds and bogs in the Northern Hemisphere, where it preys on smaller creatures, such as crustaceans, insects and larvae. It catches and digests them in the translucent bags or 'bladders' filled with water that grow on short stalks all over the plant. The largest of these is no more than $1/5$ in (5 mm) across. An opening at the front is closed by a trapdoor, hinged at the top. Branching 'antennae' diverge from either side of the door – equipped with sensitive bristles – and funnel passing creatures towards it.

Pressure is low inside the bladder. When the visitor touches one of the trap-door bristles, it trips open the seal and is caught in the flash flood gushing inwards. The suction eases and the door swings shut. Escape is impossible. The same glands are already producing the acid and enzymes that will soon dissolve the prisoner.

A TREE THAT LOOKS LIKE A SMALL FOREST

THE BANYAN TREE BRANCHES

OUT TO FORM SEPARATE TREES

When the invading soldiers of Alexander the Great passed through India they camped in the shade of a forest grove. Later, they were astounded to find it was a single tree – a giant banyan tree.

ONE-TREE GLADE *The banyan's aerial roots reach down to prop up lateral branches and extend the parent tree.*

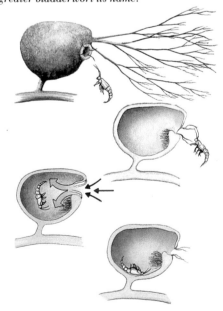

HAIR-TRIGGER TRAPS *Each bladder sucks in tiny creatures that venture too near.*

The banyan tree, *Ficus benghalensis*, starts life as a single trunk, often growing on another tree where a bird has left its seed. It then puts out wide-spreading branches which send down slender aerial rootlets that take hold of the soil to support and feed the parent branches. More and more secondary trunks take root in the same way, sometimes becoming almost as thick as the original trunk. The tree gradually spreads outwards until it forms a small forest grove of its own, capable of thriving long after the founding tree has died.

The most famous of living banyans grows in the Botanical Gardens of Calcutta, and covers an area of almost 243 acres (98 ha). A tally made on another banyan produced a count of 454 prop roots.

In India, the banyan is a sacred tree, planted near temples. Vishnu, the Hindu god, is said to have been born beneath one. In more recent times, it has been claimed that the latex produced by the tree relieves the pains of bruises and rheumatism.

THE VAMPIRE PLANT THAT FEEDS OFF ITS HOST

DODDERS AND OTHER CUSCUTA SPECIES ARE SPECIALIST PARASITES

The Jekyll and Hyde among plants, the *Cuscuta,* sometimes behaves like a normal plant, with its seed germinating in the ordinary way and putting out a root. It then, however, becomes a parasitic vampire.

Instead of feeding the young *Cuscuta,* the root merely anchors a slender stem that reaches out and sweeps the nearby area in ever-increasing circles, prospecting for a host plant. As soon as it finds one, it winds itself around it – rarely more than three times – and squeezes. This contact irritates the *Cuscuta* itself and triggers the formation of suckers that clamp down on the victim's tissues and inject damaging toxins. Soon these suckers penetrate the supply vessels of the victimised host and can tap directly into them for food and water. The *Cuscuta* now abandons its root to sponge directly off its host, living and eventually dying with the occupied plant

PARASITE TANGLE *A mass of cuscuta stems (above) swarms across the host it feeds on. Tendrils (right) have tapped into their host and are bearing flowers.*

unless it should manage to colonise other foster-plants. Curiously, if two *Cuscuta* stems meet, they coil around each other, each implanting suckers in the other, but without any effect.

All 170 known *Cuscuta* species are parasites with leaves reduced to scales. Some are specialists; others will occupy a broader choice of hosts. *Cuscuta epilinum* grows in Europe and lives solely on flax, whereas *Cuscuta epithymum*, also found in Europe and known as the common dodder, will

attack not only flax but also clover, thyme, gorse, heather, hops and nettles. *Cuscutas* cause serious damage to crops, and when they infest several plants may transmit viruses from one to another. The tobacco mosaic virus, for example, is spread by this process of poisonous transfusion.

GUESTS THAT SLOWLY STRANGLE THEIR HOSTS

FIGS IN RAIN FORESTS TAKE ROOT IN

TREES TO REACH SUNLIGHT

Fig trees love sunshine and bask in the climate of the Mediterranean, where *Ficus carica*, the edible common fig, has no competitors to put it in the shade. However, fig-tree species that live in tropical forests have to find ingenious ways of emerging from the darkness that reigns beneath a roof of trees 80-130 ft (25-40 m) tall.

Tropical figs such as *Ficus nymphaeaefolia* in Guyana and *Ficus ottoniifolia* in Gabon

VICTIM *A captive tree pokes its head above a strangler fig.*

fight long campaigns for light. They rely on the bats, birds, monkeys and other mammals that eat their fruits and disperse the seeds like rain – more than 1000 seeds per sq yd (1200 per m^2) have been counted. Only a few, however, land on sites that favour germination, which are not in the ground, but high up, near the light, on the trunks of other trees. Even then, the struggle is not over. Once they have taken root in their host, they have to reach water by sinking aerial roots into the soil beneath.

The next stage comes when the fig has grown enough to start strangling its own support. With its head facing the Sun and its feet firmly rooted in the ground, it twines more aerial root around the trunk.

The network grows denser, until the roots start to fuse together, constantly tightening their grip to constrict the flow of sap in the dying host. Yet the fig tree must be careful to balance its all-round development both in the air and on the ground. Some of its aerial roots, now thickened into pillars, may grow outwards to act as buttresses so that when the host tree eventually collapses, it will not bring down its killer.

PEACEFUL PARTNERS

SPREADING LIMBS *Cecropia branches spread their shade.*

LODGING *Cecropia and ants work for their mutual good.*

In the rain forests of Central and South America are trees that have formed a partnership with ants. Trees of the genus *Cecropia* live with colonies of *Azteca* non-stinging ants. As well as giving them shelter, the trees provide food for their lodgers, who in return evict other intruders. Outgrowths around the base of the leaves exude a mixture of protein and the carbohydrate glycogen. This does nothing for the tree, but is a key ingredient in the diet of the ants. *Cecropias* are the only plants known to produce it.

The ants have another partnership in payment for food. Inside their quarters they keep cochineal scale-insects for the sticky substance known as honeydew the insects excrete. The cochineals live on the sap of the *Cecropia*, but are not strong enough to pierce its bark. This, the ants do for them.

A TREASURY OF ANIMALS

4

TIGHT SECURITY *Huge claws let the three-toed sloth of South America hang out in safety.*

THE ANIMAL KINGDOM IS A DIVERSE AND TEEMING REALM, NATURE'S TREASURE HOUSE OF LIVING JEWELS AND ODDITIES. ITS SUBJECTS INCLUDE ABOUT 1.5 MILLION KNOWN SPECIES OF RUNNING, FLYING, SWIMMING, SLITHERING AND CRAWLING CREATURES, RANGING IN SIZE AND SHAPE FROM MINUSCULE AMOEBAE TO GIGANTIC BLUE WHALES. AND NEW SPECIES ARE BEING DISCOVERED ALL THE TIME. EACH ANIMAL IS A NATURAL MASTERPIECE, HONED TO PERFECTION TO FILL ITS PLACE IN THE NATURAL WORLD. INSECTS ARE THE MOST SUCCESSFUL. THEY OUTNUMBER HUMANS BY 12 MILLION TO ONE, THOUGH NATURALISTS HAVE ONLY IDENTIFIED AND NAMED A MILLION OF THE ESTIMATED 3 MILLION SPECIES.

OLD TIMERS *Sea urchins are among the oldest forms of life.*

STRANGE FORMS, WILD TALENTS

A newt-like creature that reproduces but never becomes

properly adult, a male 'sea horse' that carries its species'

eggs until they hatch, a fish with an electric sting in its tail

– these are some of nature's more unusual adaptations.

Nature's masterpieces can take surprising shapes and forms. The primitive, lizard-like tuatara from New Zealand, for example, is a leftover from the age of the dinosaurs. It survived the 'time of great dying' about 65 million years ago when the dinosaurs became extinct, and against all odds it still exists today. The tuatara is curious because it possesses a 'third eye' – in fact, a residual eyelid – in the top of its head. It is a 'living fossil' and thus joins the band of animals, including the sturgeon, platypus, tarsier, argonaut and pearly nautilus molluscs, garpike and paddlefish, that are survivors from another time.

Some are like the coelacanth fish – nicknamed 'old fourlegs' after the four fins on its underside – which went undetected by modern science until 1938, when one was hauled up from the depths of the Indian Ocean and recognised for what it is. It came as no surprise to fishermen of the Comoro Islands, however, who had been catching coelacanths for years. They used their skins as 'sandpaper' to rough up bicycle tyres when mending a puncture.

AUSTRALIAN ODDITY

THE STRANGE DUCKBILLED PLATYPUS
BAFFLED 18TH-CENTURY NATURALISTS

When the first duckbilled platypus was brought to London in the late 18th century, it was taken for a hoax. The animal, which comes from eastern Australia and Tasmania, was so bizarre-looking that naturalists assumed it must be a composite, assembled from bits and pieces of various other creatures.

The platypus, *Ornithorhynchus anatinus*, has a range of features that defy common ideas of what a mammal ought to look like. Instead of a snout, it has a long, duck-like bill, which – unlike a bird's – is leathery, with upturned nostrils at the end. The ears are short horizontal slits that lie just behind the small round eyes. The feet are webbed.

Its body is about 20 in (60 cm) long, and covered with short brown silky fur. It lives in long burrows by lakes and rivers, and despite its clumsy appearance is a strong swimmer. The front feet are equipped with longer webs that fold back when not in use to make it more streamlined; the back pair act as a powerful rudder.

Its internal anatomy is equally unusual. The platypus has no separate anal and genital orifices – both vent into one chamber, the cloaca, as in birds and reptiles. Although it is a mammal, the platypus lays eggs. The female usually lays two or three at a time, which she incubates for a week to ten days. The nesting chamber is a grass-and-leaf-lined cell at the end of a burrow, dug as much as 50 ft (15 m) into a riverbank.

The tiny hatchlings are pink, naked, and about 1 in (2 cm) long. They suck milk

DUCKBILLED *One of nature's oddest designs – the platypus.*

THE CARING FATHER *A male sea horse, anchored securely by the tail, houses his young in his belly pouch.*

from the female through two patches of enlarged pores in her fur, since she has no conventional teats. The young feed for about four months before they start to swim and hunt.

When fully grown, they eat bottom-dwelling water creatures, from small aquatic animals to crustaceans, frogs and insects, as well as worms, molluscs and larvae. When the platypus goes foraging in the darkness of the riverbed, both its ears and eyes are sealed tight. It is able to detect weak electrical fields produced by the muscles of its prey. It hunts at twilight and by night, collecting its catch in cheek pouches before bringing it to the surface, where it grinds its meal between a pair of horny plates – the adult platypus has no teeth.

The male is equipped with an unusual weapon for a mammal – venom glands that feed poisonous spurs on its hind ankles. The poison is enough to kill a dog or paralyse a human. The purpose of the spurs is not known, though they may be weapons the males use when fighting for dominance.

AN ELEGANT FISH WITH A HEAD LIKE A HORSE

THE SEA HORSE IS THE ONLY MALE FISH THAT GIVES BIRTH TO HIS YOUNG

In Greek mythology, the hippocampus was a creature with the forelegs of a horse and the tail of a fish. Nowadays, hippocampus describes a group of fishes whose common name 'sea horse' is uncannily appropriate. They swim in an upright position, their forward-facing heads shaped like the heads of knights in a chess set. Making the resemblance to the knight even more striking,

their bodies are covered with plates of bony armour and they have a mane of short indented spines along their backs. The creature's elongated jaws end in a small, toothless mouth that works as a valve, taking in food by suction. Its eyes move independently of one another.

The martial exterior is deceptive – sea horses are not aggressive. They swim very slowly and elegantly, using the fragile fin of their backs as a means of propulsion. To prevent them drifting while at rest or being swept away during turbulent weather, they use their tails as an anchor, curling them around seaweed or plants.

When sea horses mate, the female uses

a tubular organ to stow her eggs in an incubating pouch on the underbelly of the male, which then fertilises them. The male carries them for 50 or 60 days, providing nutrients from inside its pouch, until they hatch as small fry that can still scurry back to their father's pouch for refuge in case of an emergency.

There are about 25 species of sea horse, ranging in length from less than 2 in up to 12 in (5 to 30 cm). Some tropical species grow long bony filaments along their backs that are frilled with flaps of skin, as if draped in mantles of trailing seaweed. These particularly exotic-looking creatures are called leafy sea dragons.

SPINY DEFENCES *Australia's 'thorny devil' is a small, harmless lizard.*

Although vulnerable to fish-eaters, sea horses are poisonous to some predators, chiefly crabs. They are also able to conceal themselves by changing their colour from red to yellow or green, or by becoming translucent, according to the nature of the background.

ARMOUR-PLATED WITH SPIKES

A BRISTLING DESERT LIZARD FROM AUSTRALIA IS A PLACID ANT-EATER

In the desert interior of Australia there is a creature known by several names – the 'horned dragon', 'mountain devil' and the 'thorny devil'. If it were 50 ft (15 m) long and ferocious, it would make a terrifying monster, but in fact it is a lizard, a mere 6 in (15 cm) long and quite harmless.

The *Moloch horridus*, with its forest of sharp conical spines springing from its back, sides, limbs, nose and bulbous head, as well as its upraised and equally spiny tail, perfectly matches its alarming names. (*Horridus* means 'bristling' or 'spiky', which accounts for the origin of the word 'horror' – when people are so frightened their hair stands on end.) The lizard's spikes are extensions of the horny scales found on many reptiles as a defence against predators. In fact, the moloch is a quiet, slow-moving lizard that feeds solely on ants, lurking outside their nests to snap them up.

The moloch solved the problem of dehydration that confronts all desert-dwellers. Observers have noticed from its swallowing that even in a very arid environment it keeps drinking. It uses a network of microscopic surface canals winding around the base of its spines to drain the humidity of the sand and the morning air

that condenses on its skin and to channel this to the corners of its mouth.

Lizards often use unusually extravagant

WHERE REPTILES RULE

In Australia, unlike other parts of the world, reptiles are the chief predators. Isolated from the Eurasian continent and its advanced predatory mammals, Australia's reptiles have had few rivals. They include the largest in the world, salt-water crocodiles, over 20 ft (6 m) long. Then there are such creatures as giant monitor lizards called 'perenties' (more than 6 ft – 2 m – long), lace monitor lizards which climb trees and weigh 55 lb (25 kg) and pythons growing up to 24 ft (8 m) long. There are also bearded dragons with expandable neck-ruffs and geckos that squirt noxious fluids.

scale and spike formations for defence. The Texas horned lizard has a crown of large spikes, while the Australian bearded dragons and frilled lizards have neck-ruffs that they expand suddenly to surprise predators. Lizards of the skink family, mostly from the tropics, stick out their bright blue tongues to frighten attackers, and geckos squirt noxious fluids. When threatened, monitor lizards stand on their hind legs, blow up their necks and open their mouths wide. The tropical lizards of the Americas, basilisks, have perhaps the ultimate defence strategy: they run, not just overland but also across the surface of water, earning them the name of 'Jesus Christ lizard'.

FABULOUSLY FEATHERED

FOUR TAIL FEATHERS ARE THE GLORY OF PERU'S 'MARVELLOUS SPATULETAIL'

In the tropics, birds – especially male birds – have to compete for attention just as keenly as insects, flowers and other lifeforms do. At breeding time, in particular, there is intense competition among the males for the favours of the females, and the male with the brightest display is the most likely to win a mate.

That is why some of the finest plumage is to be found in the birds of the tropics. What makes one hummingbird from Peru, *Loddigesia mirabilis*, outstandingly conspicuous are the appendages that earn it the common name of 'marvellous spatuletail'.

Most birds have only 10 to 12 tail feathers. Some have more,

EXOTIC HUMMER *The spatuletail displays extravagant tail plumage.*

LIFE WITHOUT COLOUR

Far fewer genetic instructions are required to colour skin, scales or feathers than to shape an organ or build a bone. This helps to explain why pigmentation varies a lot, and why anomalies are common. Easily the most striking variation is

EXPOSED *No colour leaves an albino snake perilously visible.*

albinism: the more or less total absence of colour in the body covering and the iris of the eye. Albinism is found in all animal groups, including fishes, reptiles, birds, insects and mammals. When it affects species that have neither hair nor scales – some amphibians, for instance – fine blood vessels just beneath the surface may make the colourless skin look bright pink. The same thing happens in the eye, making the iris look pink.

In mammals, there are two main families of cells that make pigmentation molecules in the skin, eyes and hair follicles: the melanins are black or brown pigments that darken the site they occupy, while the carotenes are reddish-orange. A single faulty (mutant) gene can interfere with production – a lack of melanin, for example, can result in albinism, a handicap in the wild, where sufferers, conspicuous to predators and sometimes attacked for their 'strangeness' even by members of their own species, rarely survive. The albino varieties found among domesticated animals, such as some rabbits, pigeons and pet mice, result from deliberate breeding programmes.

Mating rituals, the recognition of individuals within a species, and a

KOALA IN WHITE *Albino mammals have white hair or fur and a colourless skin.*

whole range of communications and warnings are just a few of the forms of behaviour that depend on pigmentation. Pigments also protect the skin and eyes against sunlight, and many animals use them for protective coloration.

ALL EYES AND FINGERS *In its nocturnal habitat, Asia's deceptively timid-looking spectral tarsier is a fierce small-scale carnivore.*

reduced to single filaments. Loud calls and bright plumage advertise his presence to local hens, and when they arrive he starts his courtship parade. He bounces around displaying to his prospective mate, and then sidles up to her and tickles her under the chin with his tail. The feathers are flicked from side to side in an arousing twist-like dance until the female succumbs.

UPRIGHT SLEEPER ON A TREE TRUNK

WIDE-OPEN, INNOCENT EYES DISGUISE
A PREDATORY PRIMATE

The huge, brown, saucer-like eyes of the spectral tarsier, *Tarsius spectrum,* dominate its face and are larger than its brain. They are designed to catch the tiniest glimmer of light – essential in a nocturnal creature – and enable it to judge distances with great accuracy when leaping from tree to tree. Such a winsomely innocent appearance, however, fails to mirror the creature's predatory behaviour and territorial habits.

The tarsiers of South-east Asia belong to an unusual suborder of primates, the prosimians, who also include the similarly large-eyed lorises, also found in South-east Asia, India and Sri Lanka, and the lemurs of Madagascar. Tarsiers have bodies up to 7 in (18 cm) long and tails that measure over 10 in (25 cm). With hind legs proportionally longer than in any other primate, they are amazing athletes, and can easily leap five times their body length from a standing start on a tree.

They owe their name to the extreme length of their tarsal bones – the bones in the heel and ankle region. On the tips of their exceptionally long, thin fingers and toes they have fleshy pads, rather like the suction pads of frogs' feet, that help them to cling fast to tree trunks and branches. They can then rest in their characteristic upright posture, their long legs folded up to their shoulders and their outstretched tails pressed against a tree trunk to help them to keep their balance.

Although tarsiers cannot move their forward-facing eyes, they have an uncanny ability to swivel their heads through 180°,

such as pheasants with 32, but the marvellous spatuletail lies at the other extreme. Hanging from a body 1⅕ in (3 cm) long are four tail feathers. What it lacks in quantity it makes up for in quality. The feathers are proportionally very long – about 3⅓ in (11 cm), more than three times the body length – and the two outer feathers are shorn of barbs except at the ends, where they form a symmetrical paddle shape. These feathers cross over twice, both at the base of the tail and in the middle, and can be brought smartly together during flight with a loud slap.

Another small bird with an unusual tail is the wired-tailed manakin of Venezuela. The male has brightly coloured head and neck feathers, lustrous black wings and a tail with feathers that are very long but

ANCIENT AND MODERN: SURVIVORS FROM THE DEPTHS OF TIME

Palaeontologists, students of fossils and life's most ancient forms, measure history in tens and hundreds of millions of years. For them, most of the animal species that share this planet are 'modern' – the average life span of all the species that ever lived being about 4 million years. Nevertheless, several living species have features that are remarkably similar to those of far-distant ancestors.

For example, the sphenodon (*Sphenodon punctatus*), a lizard-like reptile about 24 in (60 cm) long, known by its Maori name of tuatara and found on a few rocky islands in New Zealand, is a 'relic species'. It is the sole survivor of a once-flourishing group, Sphenodontian, that first appeared in the Triassic period about 230 million years ago, alongside the earliest dinosaurs. Animals like the tuatara existed

SURVIVOR *The tuatara is New Zealand's oldest inhabitant.*

about 60 million years ago.

Even more ancient and extraordinary-looking is the coelacanth, *Latimeria chalumnae*, a fish that grows nearly 6 ft (180 cm) long and weighs up to 210 lb (95 kg). It belongs to a group, the Coelacanthini, that was last seen in the fossil record 80 million years ago. The group was thought to be extinct until a South African fisherman found something spectacular in the catch of his trawler in 1938 and showed it to the local scientist and museum curator, Marjorie Courtenay-Latimer. Later investigations indicated that this particular fish had strayed a long way from its species' home territory, near the Comoro Islands in the Indian Ocean.

Coelacanths are members of the 'lobe-fin' group of fishes that first appeared more than 400 million

LIVE FOSSIL *The coelacanth belongs to a group that is over 400 million years old.*

years ago. These gave rise to 'lung-fishes', which went ashore some 370 million years ago and founded the line of four-legged creatures that

led to humans. The coelacanths stayed at sea, and their descendant, *Latimeria*, with its armoured scales, two dorsal fins and paired front fins, gives an authentic glimpse of an age long gone.

A still more primitive 'living fossil', the common horseshoe crab, *Limulus polyphemus*, dwells on North America's eastern coast. It is not a crab at all, but descended from a group of jawless fossil arthropods called Xiphosurida, which are classed as arachnids, together with spiders, mites and scorpions. They are the closest living relatives

of trilobites – extinct invertebrates.

Four other species of horseshoe crab live on the Pacific coast of Asia, proving that these crabs, unlike the coelacanth, are still vigorous and widespread some 420 million years after their first appearance in the Silurian period.

SPIDER CRAB *Horseshoe 'crabs' belong to the same class as spiders.*

Other reminders of an earlier era include species that are so familiar it seems extraordinary that they have been around for so long. Dragonflies and cockroaches are long-established groups, with recognisable ancestors preserved in rocks more than 400 million years old. Likewise, the simple and obviously efficient anatomy of sharks and rays has hardly changed since they first came on the scene 370 million years ago.

and their great agility, coupled with their keen vision and acute hearing, make them successful predators on small animals – from insects and worms to reptiles such as geckos, birds, frogs, young mammals and even crabs and fish. They live alone or in pairs, bringing up one infant at a time within a small area.

Tarsius spectrum lives on the Indonesian island of Sulawesi (Celebes) and other nearby islands. Of the two other tarsier species, *Tarsius bancanus* (Horsfield's tarsier) lives in Borneo, Sumatra and neighbouring islands, and *Tarsius syrichta* (the Philippines tarsier) in the Philippines. The group is now quite rare, but the skeletons of very similar-looking primates have been found that date from more than 35 million years ago. Some experts believe that tarsiers were once plentiful in Eurasia and North America, but that they were driven out by their cousins, the monkeys, and retreated to these last few island outposts.

MINIATURE LACEMAKERS

THE INDUSTRIOUS SPIDER WEAVES
WEBS OF EXTRAORDINARY DELICACY

The delicate lacework of a spider's web is the labour of one of nature's most outstanding artisans. The fine silk thread, with a diameter of $^1/_{5000}$ in (0.002 mm), is

TAKING THE INITIATIVE *The web-caster spider, from the genus* Dinopis, *does not wait for visitors. Instead, it aims small webs at passing prey.*

stronger than a similar-sized strand of steel and is also extraordinarily elastic – capable of stretching by a third of its length without snapping.

The silk is produced in a

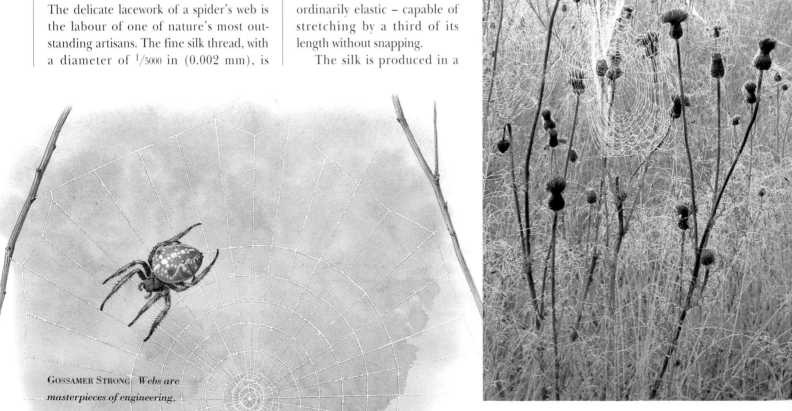

GOSSAMER STRONG *Webs are masterpieces of engineering.*

SUN AND DEW *Orb-web spiders adorn whole meadows with fine tracery (left). Monkey spiders (right) are ground-dwellers, living in silk-lined burrows.*

number of glands within the spider's abdomen. These secrete a fluid rich in protein through three pairs of passages or 'spinnerets' just in front; this then hardens as a resilient thread. Depending on the silk gland used, a spider can manufacture a range of threads: a fairly coarse type, for example, for the basic structure of the web; a sticky thread to bind the prey; and a thicker type to spin the cocoon that holds the eggs. Young spiders spin a finer gossamer thread to float them on the wind in search of new territories. No single spider produces every one of the seven different kinds of silk that exist, but many manufacture three or four varieties.

The familiar orb webs, built up in concentric circles of geometrical precision, are spun in the shelter of doorways or hedges by spiders of the Argiopidae family. The more complex web system of the banded argiope, *Argiope bruennechi*, is found in tall grasses in open country. Yet the circular design is only one of a much wider range. The mobile retiarius or net-casting spider, from any of several species of *Dinopis*, instead of passively waiting for dinner to drop in, spins a small, sticky rectangular web that it holds in its forelimbs and casts over passing prey. Trapdoor spiders live in holes in the ground that they line with silk and conceal behind camouflaged earthen doors that swing on silken hinges. The spitting spiders of the Scytodidae family trap insects by squirting a jet of silk at them.

WINTER PRECAUTIONS THAT COMBAT FREEZING

COPPER BUTTERFLY CATERPILLARS

HAVE THEIR OWN ANTIFREEZE

The caterpillar of the scarce copper butterfly, *Heodes virgaureae*, is one of the few living creatures that can survive temperatures close to $-38°C$ ($-36°F$).

In the more temperate reaches of its European and central Asian homeland, the copper lives in mountain areas; in the subarctic regions, it lives on grasslands. To counter the extreme winter cold of its habitat, the larva produces its own glycerol, one of the components used to

LIVING IN SILK *A hinged silk door conceals the burrow of a trapdoor spider. Some species have teeth adapted for digging.*

ANTIFREEZE *Larvae of the rare copper butterfly have an antifreeze system to protect them during harsh winters.*

make antifreeze for motor car radiators. This lowers the freezing point of the body fluid to –15°C (5°F); it also increases its viscosity or stickiness, further reducing the freezing point to –38°C (–36°F). Produced before or during hibernation, and shed after winter eases, the glycerol may account for as much as 40 per cent of the caterpillar's total weight.

In the Arctic, hairy caterpillars of the *Gynaephora* moth have a different strategy to survive the cold. They are 'freeze tolerant'. Instead of using antifreeze in the blood, they reduce the amount of water in the body and avoid cell damage during freezing. The drawback is that they take 13 years to pupate – that is, become pupa, the intermediate stage between the larva and

THE PETER PAN SALAMANDER

In some animals, perpetual youth is not a vain dream but a survival tactic. It is practised by many urodele amphibians – that is, the newts and salamanders – including the axolotl, *Ambystoma mexicanum*. This 8 in (20 cm) salamander is found only in a few high-altitude lakes in Mexico. All amphibians pass through a larval (tadpole) stage, when they live mostly in water and breathe through their gills, before changing into an air-breathing form that enables them to spend time on land. The axolotl, however, usually keeps the juvenile form, complete with gills, throughout its life and never leaves the water. This may be caused by a lack of iodine in the local water that affects the production of hormones controlling growth. Or it could be that the lake is too cold for the hormones to be effective. Either way, missing out on the full adult form has enabled the species to survive in otherwise inhospitable conditions. No one realised that the axolotl was a salamander until 1865, when some specimens taken to Paris mysteriously metamorphosed into the previously unknown adult form.

When a sexually mature adult retains larval features in this way, it is known as neoteny. Scientists who believe that birds are descended from small dinosaurs called theropods have suggested that neoteny may have been responsible. Juvenile theropods may have developed temporary feathers, just as baby elephants grow thick woolly coats to keep them warm. If having feathers enabled them to glide, thereby improving their chances of survival, the logic of evolution would have encouraged the adults to keep them. What started as a means of insulation became even more useful as a means of locomotion.

PINK FRILLS *The juvenile gills of the axolotl salamander are so useful that it cannot afford to lose them and grow up.*

the fully blown adult. They spend most of their larval life in the deep-freeze, only thawing out during the brief summer, when they feed and grow.

Two species of bumble bee are another of the Arctic's special adaptations. They are first into the air each spring because they are able to vibrate their flight muscles and generate heat to keep their body up to 16°C (60°F) above the icy air temperature.

SHOCKING FISHES

ELECTRIC EELS GENERATE 600 VOLT
CHARGES WITH THEIR MUSCLES

All muscle activity is triggered by electrical impulses, but only a few animals have taken this connection further, modifying some muscles so thoroughly that instead of contracting they generate a current. The electric eel, *Electrophorus electricus,* produces a series of brief discharges, each lasting about two-thousandths of a second, with a maximum output of more than 600 volts.

This organic battery can stun any small animal nearby, and can even knock out a mammal the size of a horse. In 1941, two Brazilian workers who fell into an aquarium containing electric eels were killed instantly.

The electric eel is not a true eel but a South American freshwater fish that was given its name because of its elongated body – up to 8¼ ft (2.5 m) long, four-fifths of it tail. It is the lower half of the tail muscle that carries the main electrical cell, but the eel also has two others: one of them working with the main cell, the other generating an electric field around the fish. The electric eel has a special organ that is sensitive to any minute disturbances in this field, and can thereby detect the presence of other life forms that cause them. Adult electric eels eventually lose the use of their eyes – which serve for little in the murky river conditions – so this 'radar' ability is vital to their survival.

When prey is detected, the electric eel discharges its battery to stun or kill, but it cannot repeat the shock before a long rest and plenty of food have restored the energy it used up in a fraction of a second.

Unlike the electric eel, the electric catfish, *Malapterurus electricus,* found in the River Nile and parts of central Africa, has excellent vision. It grows to a length of over 3 ft (1 m) and produces a discharge of 100 volts from a layer of tissue located just beneath the skin and covering all of its body except for the head.

Some marine fishes can also generate electrical power. These include the star-gazers of southern seas, so called because they live in the sand with their eyes turned upwards. Electric rays or torpedoes have generating cells located in the 'wings' (pectoral fins) at each side of their heads. These can put out more than 200 volts – enough to floor a human being.

POWER TO ELECTROCUTE *Electric eels use high-voltage shocks to stun, and sometimes even kill, their foes.*

ARMS AND ARMOUR

Kill or be killed is the law of the wild. Many animals have evolved ingenious protective measures to save them from instant termination – from armour-plated coats, to detachable spears, to pre-emptive chemical weapons.

Animals have many ways of dealing with predators. They run for their lives, hide away in safe places, or stand firm. The ones who stand their ground usually do so knowing that they have substantial defences to call on. Some wear armoured coats; others deploy chemical weapons, and a third contingent rely on appearing to be more dangerous than they really are. They include slow-moving animals, such as hermit crabs and the pangolins (or scaly anteaters) of Africa and Asia, well protected with scales or shells. Millipedes exude the poisonous gas hydrogen cyanide from the pores along their long, segmented bodies and guarantee themselves a safe passage.

The predators, however, try to keep one step ahead of their prey. The ingenious bombardier beetle successfully deters frogs, ants and other beetle-eating predators with a chemical defence system, but the garden spider is able to wrap it in a silk cocoon. Inside this, the trapped beetle discharges its chemical gun harmlessly and the spider savours its meal uninterrupted.

ARMOUR-PLATED PACIFISTS

TORTOISES AND TURTLES ARE AMONG THE BEST-DEFENDED OF ALL CREATURES

The Roman army invented a defensive formation in which a group of legionaries under attack held overlapping shields facing outwards on all sides and above their heads. They called it *testudo* – tortoise – in honour of the reptile with the most efficient armour worn by any land vertebrate of the Earth's more recent history.

A tortoise's armour is double-walled throughout. On the outside, the 'carapace' is a shock-resistant layer consisting of big semi-flexible horny plates or 'scutes'; inside, a thick shell of bony plates reinforces the structure. The two are joined at the edges, with openings at the front and back large enough for the head, limbs and tail. In an emergency, the occupant can withdraw every organ vulnerable to an attacker inside its fortress. The different plates of the shell are part of the skeleton and grow as the tortoise grows.

SAFETY FIRST *The giant tortoise of the Galápagos Islands is too heavy to run, but too solid to need to.*

NINE-BANDED ARMADILLO *Bony plates cover this American mammal from head to tail.*

The most complete and solid shells belong to land tortoises – the Testudinidae family – whose generally high-domed shells make them hard for a predator to grasp. The flatter shells of aquatic turtles, on the other hand, make them more streamlined when they swim, but often more vulnerable.

Some turtles have shed their horny plates. Much the largest living turtle, for example, is the ocean-going leatherback turtle, *Dermochelys coriacea* – weighing up to 110 stone (700 kg). Its carapace consists of a mosaic of pieces of tough leathery skin and small bony plaques, with no horny scutes. The largest known Pacific leatherback was a colossal 8 ft 4 in (2.5 m) long. Nobody knows for sure how long these turtles live, but most almost certainly reach the age of 50, and some may even be more than 100 years old.

ARMOURED MAMMALS

PANGOLINS AND SOME ARMADILLOS
ROLL UP INTO A BALL FOR SAFETY

The giant pangolin looks more like some prehistoric reptile than a mammal, with its back, legs, head and tail clad in pointed, overlapping scales. But the hair growing between the scales, around its snout and

ANGLED BLADES *The scales of the coiled pangolin are sharp enough to slice a questing paw.*

on its belly classifies it as a mammal, and the females suckle their young as with other mammals, too. The horny scales are flexible at birth, but by the following day they have hardened to a consistency tough enough to have a cutting edge. When the animal rolls up to protect its vulnerable belly, it bristles like a pine cone, its scales standing erect and intimidating predators.

The giant pangolin is the largest of seven species: four of them from tropical Africa; the others found in parts of Southeast Asia, including Malaya, Java and southern China. All are specialised ant and termite-

BACK FOLDED WITH HEAD LOCKED NEXT TO TAIL *When attacked, a three-banded armadillo curls up into a neatly jointed sphere.*

eaters, with a keen sense of smell to locate the insects, powerful claws to root them out of their nests, and long sticky tongues to catch them. They scrape the ants off with the horny ridges of their mouths.

Pangolins are an evolutionary puzzle because naturalists know little about their ancestry or their relationships with other mammals. For some time, they were thought to be related to the anteaters of South America, which have the same diet and look roughly similar, with long snouts and tongues, claws and long nails – though the anteaters have fur rather than armour. In fact, these similarities are a classic example of 'convergent evolution' – the tendency of totally unrelated animals to 'converge' on an ideal design that helps them to survive, and also makes them look alike. For example, sharks, which are fish, share their streamlined shapes with killer whales, which are mammals, and with the extinct ichthyosaurus, which was a seagoing reptile of the Mesozoic era – about 65 million years ago. All these big marine predators reached similar designs for rapid swimming.

The armadillo of Central and South America is another well-protected mammal. Fortunately for its mother, its skin is particularly soft at birth, but within a few days it has hardened into many small armour plates. Arranged in overlapping bands around the

THE 'QUEEN OF GEMS'

The pearl results from an accident of nature. It forms when a foreign body – a grain of sand or some small dead parasite – gets stuck in the soft body cells of some bivalve molluscs, in particular oysters of the genus *Pinctada* and mussels of the genus *Unio*. To protect itself against the irritating intruder, the mantle (outer tissue) of the mollusc deposits alternate layers of nacre, or mother-of-pearl, and conchiolin (a horny protein-rich compound) around it to make it more 'comfortable'.

The resulting pearl is usually irregular in shape, though the closer

GEM *Grit becomes a pearl inside the oyster.*

it comes to a perfect sphere, the more it is prized by people. A pearl's lustre comes from light reflecting and refracting among the layers of

nacre. The world's largest pearl oyster beds are in the Persian Gulf and Red Sea, off north-west Sri Lanka and Australia, and around the islands of the South Pacific. One of the largest-ever natural pearls belonged to a 19th-century London banker, Henry Thomas Hope, and weighed over 10 oz (280 g).

trunk, these shield the head and shoulders and, in some species, the legs and tail; the stripes of soft skin in between the bands allow the armadillo to flex its body. The nine-banded long-nosed armadillo, *Dasypus novemcinctus* (the only armadillo species found in the United States), can actually have as many as eleven bands; it weighs between 9 and 18 lb (4 to 8 kg) and is 15 to 17 in (38 to 43 cm) long.

When threatened by predators, some species of armadillo curl up in self-defence, but only the three-banded armadillo, *Tolypeutes matacus*, is able to roll itself into a ball.

MYTHICAL MONSTERS

GIANT CLAMS – BENIGN MOLLUSCS
THAT LIVE AMONG CORAL REEFS

Hollywood adventure movies have given the giant clam an awesome reputation, with deep-sea divers struggling to free themselves from jaws that have snapped shut like a steel trap in the midst of a coral reef. But the truth is less dramatic: the fluted valves of the giant clam close far too slowly to trap even a snail's-pace diver.

Their function is protection (clamping shut to prevent the mollusc from drying out when temporarily stranded above the water line, for example), not aggression. The giant clam feeds not by trapping passers-by but by filtering tiny organisms from the water. Even the dimensions of

HARMLESS MONSTER *A giant clam absorbs drifting particles from the sea through its feeding 'siphon'.*

WALKING STOCKADE *Few animals risk the painful injuries inflicted by a porcupine's springy spines.*

the giant clam are often exaggerated – exceptional specimens rarely exceed about 3 ft (1 m) in length and 440 lb (200 kg) in weight.

The giant clam is certainly a monster when compared with tiny bivalve relatives, such as *Nucula*, found off the coast of the Yucatán peninsula in Mexico and measuring just 1/32 in (1 mm) across. In both cases, as with all molluscs, the shell is made of calcium carbonate and defends its owner in two ways. First, it gives protection against predators such as fish, crustaceans, marine worms, starfish and other molluscs, including some that secrete acids capable

of eating their way through shells. Second, it gives shelter against natural forces, including the rise and fall of tides and differences in temperature.

PRICKLY ADVERSARIES

*ROWS OF FEARSOME QUILLS ARE THE
PORCUPINE'S SAFETY MEASURE*

Legend once had it that the porcupine of Africa, Asia, south-east Europe and America defended itself by shooting its quills like arrows – a mistaken belief probably based on observations of lions or leopards with quills embedded in their snouts or paws following a painful confrontation with this prickly opponent. Porcupines (genus *Hystrix*) are big rodents – the largest weigh up to 66 lb (30 kg) – with strong, sharp

quills up to 16 in (40 cm) long on their backs and tails. They do not 'shoot' their quills, but the quills detach themselves easily from the skin.

These black-and-white banded quills mean that porcupines are among the best-protected of all mammals. When a porcupine feels threatened, it makes its quills stand on end and rattles them together as a warning. If the threat persists, it turns its back on its enemy and then runs into it in reverse. This drives away the assailant, or stabs it full of quills. Only leopards have a keen enough appetite to risk serious injury by trying to deliver a swift blow to the porcupine's head and turning the creature on its back to get at its unprotected belly.

This type of protection is not uncommon in the animal world and is found, for

PUFFED OUT AND BRISTLING
*A threatened porcupine fish
becomes a ball of poisonous spines.
The wounds the spines inflict can
take a long time to heal.*

example, in sea urchins (Echinus), and in fishes such as the scorpion fish (family Scorpaenidae) and porcupine fish (family Diodonidae). The best-known of prickly animals are hedgehogs, like the European hedgehog, *Erinaceus europaeus*. A nocturnal insect-eater related to moles and shrews, the hedgehog is also immune to the venom of the snakes that form another part of its diet.

INFLATION AS A DEFENCE

*THE PORCUPINE FISH SWALLOWS WATER
AND TURNS INTO A BALL OF SPIKES*

The peaceful diodon, *Diodon hystrix*, spends most of its time quietly browsing on coral and small crustaceans. A sluggish swimmer, it would make a sitting target for predators, but for the fact that it is covered with a mass of strong bony spines that have earned it the names of porcupine fish and sea hedgehog.

Usually the spines are flush with the skin, but when the diodon is alarmed it will suddenly inflate its body to three times its normal size – like puffer fish – rapidly gulping air or water to fill its stomach. The diodon then rises to the surface, presenting

the alarming sight of a large spiky ball. Unwary predators soon sheer off – the poisonous spines inflict painful wounds that take a long time to heal. The diodon may grow up to 28 in (70 cm) long.

BEETLES THAT USE CHEMICAL WARFARE

*JETS OF PAINFUL GAS DETER ENEMIES
OF THE BOMBARDIER BEETLE*

The bombardier beetle, as *Brachinus crepitans* is commonly known, is an apt description of an insect with an astute means of defence. It is a ground beetle that shares a special weapon with some of its relatives in the family of carnivorous carabid beetles. When attacked this enables it to expel a jet of irritant brown gas, sometimes smelling like iodine, with a crackling sound. The crackling takes aggressors by surprise,

CHEMICAL WARFARE
*A bombardier beetle fires off a
defensive shot of toxic spray.*

and the gas blinds them temporarily, allowing the beetle to make good its escape. *Crepitans* is Latin for 'cracking'.

The secret of this weapon lies in two glands at the rear of the beetle's abdomen. It uses a technique, practised in human chemical warfare in the 20th century, of storing two different chemicals that are harmless by themselves, but dangerous when combined. The first contains a solution whose active ingredients are 25 per cent oxygenated water and 10 per cent hydroquinone (an aromatic compound, also often found in plants); the second contains the enzyme peroxidase, which is manufactured by both plants and animals. In the case of the bombardier beetle, the reaction between the compounds is explosive, generating a temperature of 100°C (212°F). The beetle expels an irritant cloud of steam and quinone in successive bursts.

It is like the firing of a machine gun – in other words, not a spray but a series of rapid pulses. If the beetle produced a continuous spray the temperature and force of the explosion would blow off its own hindquarters. Instead, the pulsed effect lets the explosion chamber cool between blasts.

Other similar beetles have their own weapons systems. There is a metriine beetle that just oozes boiling poison from under its wing-cases, surrounding itself in a noxious froth. And there is a paussine

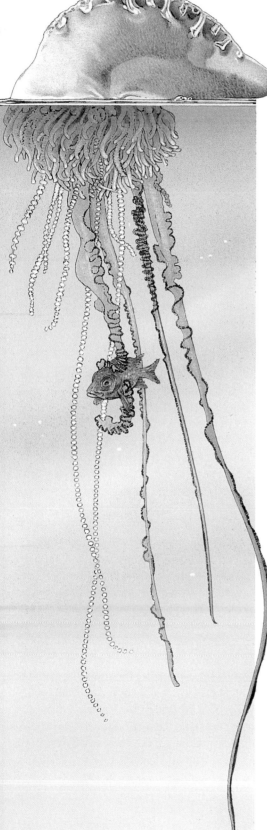

COLONY AT WAR *A Portuguese
man-of-war holds a small fish
helpless in its tentacles.*

beetle, *Goniotripis*, which employs a common principle of physics when firing gases. When milk is poured from a jug it has a tendency to curl around the lip and dribble on to the tablecloth. This is known as the 'Coanda effect' – the tendency for liquids or gases to follow the curve of a solid. In the case of the beetle, there is a flange on either side of the abdomen that acts as a deflector, like the lip of the milk jug. By twisting the abdomen slightly, the beetle can aim to the side or rear.

DANGEROUS COLONY OF FLOATING LIFE-FORMS

*THE PORTUGUESE MAN-OF-WAR'S
TENTACLES PARALYSE WITH PAIN*

A Portuguese man-of-war (*Physalia*) looks like a large jellyfish, although it belongs to a completely different biological class, the hydrozoas. And like a jellyfish, it can be a menace to swimmers. Cases of fatal poisoning are rare, but contact with one of its tentacles produces vicious burning and a whiplash mark.

The man-of-war is really a colony of life-forms, none of which can survive on its own and each of which has its own specialised function: floating, capturing prey, digestion of the prey or reproduction. The most visible parts are the inflatable bladders, up to 12 in (30 cm) long. Filled with gas, these enable men-of-war to float or submerge, and even act as sails when the wind blows – they are their only means of controlling movement. Other members of the colony, called gastrozooids, provide its 'communal' mouth and stomach, and others again, the gonozooids, make the eggs or sperm.

But the lethal reputation of the Portuguese man-of-war comes from its hunter-killer components – a mass of tentacles called dactylozooids, that are like fishing lines up to 165 ft (50 m) long and armed all along with stinging cells. These cells are like tiny harpoons that fire on contact and inject nerve poisons powerful enough to paralyse the heart of the fish

they prey on. The tentacles can contract to a seventieth of their full length in order to reel in their victims, which are digested and shared as nourishment with the rest of the colony.

True jellyfish can be just as dangerous as Portuguese men-of-war. The infamous sea wasps or box jellyfish found in the seas around Australia and the Philippines are considered to be among the most venomous animals in the world. The poison from stinging cells on their tentacles can kill people in under ten minutes by paralysing their nerves and muscles. Box jellyfish may be encountered singly or, at certain times of the year, in great swarms. Australian lifeguards have taken to wearing 'pantihose' in the water to reduce the chances of being stung.

LETHAL WEAPON

*TERMITES SQUIRT A DEADLY GLUE TO
PARALYSE AND KILL ATTACKING ANTS*

No sooner do ants attacking termites' nests start to advance than soldier termites mount their own counter-attack. Some of the 2000 species of termite bite their foes to inject them with poisonous compounds; others brush poisons on to them. But the species *Nasutus* has an altogether different, though no less deadly, weapon.

Its soldiers are blind, with tiny jaws, but they are also equipped with big frontal glands that secrete a gluey substance, together with a set of tubes to squirt it with. The enemy – usually an ant, and larger

GLUE-SQUIRTING WARRIORS
Soldier termites of the species
Nasutus *defend their nest in the
rain forest of Costa Rica.*

MASK OF FEAR *Snake's-head markings disguise a harmless Madagascan caterpillar.*

BRIGHT DEFENCES *Sea slugs' lurid colours warn off enemies.*

than the soldier termite – finds its legs and antennae hopelessly enmeshed in a sticky thread $2/5$ to $1^1/5$ in (1 to 3 cm) long, and dies paralysed and asphyxiated. Ants touched by, but not entangled with, the termites' glue may still die in contortions within 30 seconds.

One danger is when the target is too close: the *Nasutus* soldier sometimes gets caught in the grip of its own sticky thread, and dies with the enemy.

A POISONOUS DEFENCE

SEA SLUGS USE OTHER CREATURES' POISON FOR THEIR OWN DEFENCE

Sea slugs are molluscs, belonging to the same biological class as snails and limpets, but they have no trace of a shell. Since they prey on anemones, sponges and corals, this

nakedness would have made them extremely vulnerable to other predators had they not developed a subtle means of protection. Cells in their skin contain a permanent supply of sulphuric acid; if attacked, the cell walls break and release the poisonous acid.

Some sea slugs have an extra weapon in their arsenal – a stolen one. Feeding on sea anemones, corals, jellyfish and even the deadly Portuguese man-of-war, they absorb the stinging cells (nematocysts) from their prey without peril to themselves. The victims discharge about half their stinging cells as they are eaten but the rest are diverted to sacs opening off the digestive gland and stored in the secondary breathing organs, known as 'ceratia', positioned on the sea slugs' backs. Any attacker that touches the ceratia, but lacks their new owner's immunity system, suffers painful consequences.

Many species of sea slug are adorned with frills, ruffles and tendrils, all in vivid colours. Thanks to these organic works of art, they have acquired colourful names such as Haitian jewel snail (*Micromelo undata*), pyjama nudibranch (*Chromodoris quadricolor*) and flamingo-tongue snail (*Cyphoma gibbosa*). Their brilliance may act as warning signals to remind would-be predators of their hidden defences.

A CATERPILLAR THAT TERRIFIES BABOONS

CATERPILLARS SCARE OFF PREDATORS WITH SNAKE-LIKE COLOURINGS

An American expert on the behaviour of primates, G.A.K. Marshall, once confronted two of his research baboons with a caterpillar of the Madagascan butterfly

Hippotion orisiris. At the sight of this creeping monster, the frightened monkeys jumped for the nearest roof – thinking that it was a snake.

Towards the front end of its body, the so-called snake caterpillar has two 'ocelli' – that is, eye-like patches of concentric colours – which enable it to mimic the head of a snake. When the caterpillar feels in any way threatened, it simply inflates its thorax and displays its huge false eyes. At the same time, it sways its body like a snake in order to drive off birds, lizards and other predators.

Some caterpillars also have markings on the underside of their bodies that mimic the gaping lower jaw of a snake, and they swell them up when needs be in serpentine threat. In fact, it is the ability to frighten that matters more than a strict resemblance to any particular animal – in Madagascar, for example, there are no adders or other poisonous snakes.

Other caterpillars have equally deterrent designs. For instance, the caterpillar of the puss moth (*Cerura vinula*), native to Europe and Asia, can puff up its head to mimic a red-faced, black-eyed monster. Adding to the effect is a circular mouth also outlined in black.

In the wild, the eyes of a keen-sighted carnivore spell danger to other animals. That is why moths and butterflies throughout the world are equipped with false eyes, or ocelli, sometimes with a pair on each wing. Even certain fishes have them to mimic predators.

Not all ocelli are designed to be threats, however. Sometimes they divert a predator, encouraging it to attack a less vulnerable part of a butterfly. One Malaysian butterfly, for example, has what appears to be a head and antenna sketched out on its rear wings. A predator attacks, only to find it has taken an insignificant part of the butterfly's wings; this allows the insect to escape fatal injury, at least once.

Black and yellow stripes are another deterrent. Predators associate this color combination with wasps and hornets and tend to avoid prey with like markings. The alder moth caterpillar adopts this strategy

KALEIDOSCOPIC WARNINGS

Some animals use colour as a means of camouflaging themselves in their environment. For others, however, it is a way of signalling danger. Some reptiles, insects, amphibians and fishes, for example, adopt gaudy colours that

STAY AWAY! *The salamander's spots act like warning lights.*

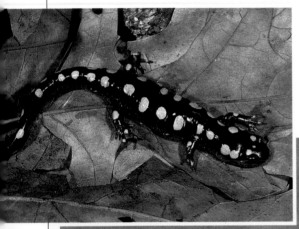

cry out to hungry passers-by: 'Stop, stay away, I am dangerous to meddle with!' Most of these loud dressers have unpleasant surprises in store for whoever ignores the warning: a venomous bite or a sting, toxic skin, foul smells or sprays.

The small frogs that inhabit the rain forests of Central and South America are particularly dramatic. Various species are coloured in opalescent shades of turquoise or green, mottled with blobs and streaks of black. The body of *Dendrobates pumilio* is vermilion, its legs

black speckled with sky blue – like a piece of pottery with a deep metallic glaze. These beautiful skins proclaim that the frogs are deadly poisonous. Indeed, the whole family is known as arrow-poison frogs, since the region's tribal inhabitants extract their toxic secretions and use them on arrowheads to paralyse birds and monkeys.

With its bright yellow patches on a black background, the spotted salamander, *Salamandra maculosa*, also warns careless consumers that glands in its skin produce poisons. The shield bug or stinkbug, *Graphosoma italicum*, has a symmetrical livery of smart

black and red stripes that gives fair warning of its foul smell.

The purpose of these vivid colorations is clear: they ward off attackers. If, however, predators are undeterred by the colours, they will still learn a lesson. They may lose their lives or they may have a painful experience. In future, such animals will associate a particular colour or pattern with the pain that comes with it, and steer clear of trouble.

A LETHAL BEAUTY *An arrow-poison frog displays the vivid hues that herald death for an attacker. The shield bug (inset) flaunts similarly loud patterns.*

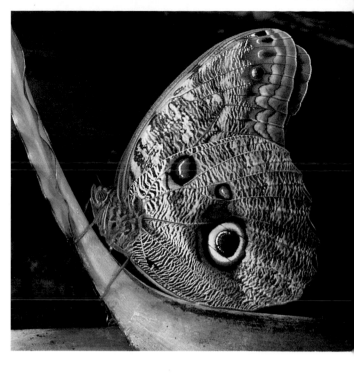

during its development. At first, it mimics the hues of a bird dropping – an equally repulsive colour – but later dons a protective black and yellow coat.

A BUTTERFLY'S OWLISH, WATCHING EYE

PAINTED EYES ON THEIR WINGS KEEP OWL BUTTERFLIES SAFE

The sight of a pair of large, watching eyes gazing up at them is enough to put many would-be predators off the owl butterflies of South America. The *Caligo* species, which live deep in the continent's rain forests, owe their name to a feathered pattern and huge eyespots that look very much like an owl's head sketched out on the underside of each hind wing.

They are large butterflies, with a wingspan of 4 to 4³/4 in (10 to 12 cm), and are active mainly at dusk, beneath the canopy of the rain forest's trees. Here, their neutral colouring attracts little attention from predators. During the daytime, the insects rest with their wings folded up above their backs, with the ocellus (false eye) displayed

FALSE COLOURS *The harmless king snake mimics the uniform of its deadly fellow, the coral snake.*

UNBLINKING EYE *An owl butterfly's hind wing reveals a yellow iris and dark pupil.*

on each side to frighten off any possible attackers – mainly birds that have good reason to fear owls.

Other moths and butterflies use a different technique. Instead of keeping their eyespots permanently displayed, they snap open their wings or twitch their forewings – depending on where the eyespots are positioned. This impression of flickering or blinking gives their enemies the uneasy feeling that they are in the watchful presence of a much larger animal lurking in the gloom.

KILLER COLOURS FOR KING SNAKES

KING SNAKES COPY THE COLOURINGS OF MORE LETHAL SERPENTS

Why should one snake disguise itself as a member of a completely different species of snake? American king snakes, such as the California mountain king snake

(*Lampropeltis zonata*) and the milk snake (*Lampropeltis triangulum*), are slim, agile predators, about 5 to 6¹/2 ft (1.5 to 2 m) long. They kill small animals, such as rats, mice, lizards and other snakes, by coiling round them and choking them in the same way as a constrictor. They are fortunate enough to be immune to the venom of other snakes, such as copperheads and rattlesnakes, but since they have no venom of their own they are vulnerable to hunting birds and mammals.

Their solution to this problem is to become mimics, copying the markings of the Americas' extremely venomous and universally feared coral snakes of the genus *Micrurus*. These have warning bands of black, yellow, red, yellow and black again, in that order. Some king snakes mimic the coral snake's warning bands well enough to keep predators at a safe distance. The king snake's bands are slightly different – coloured black, yellow, black, red and black again. But they are near enough to deceive animals, though not humans – hence the useful folk rhyme:

Red and black, friend of Jack.
Red and yella', kill a fella'.

THE ART OF CAMOUFLAGE

of its fur enables it to merge with the leaves, branches and dappled sunlight in the undergrowth. From its hidden position the tiger is able to creep up on or ambush unsuspecting prey. Similarly, a young deer with mottled brown or spotted fur can lie motionless in the vegetation and avoid being spotted by a hungry tiger.

Camouflage is not confined to the higher animals, since 'cryptic colouring' of one sort or another is used by all kinds of creatures to gain a meal or to stay off the menu of another creature. The simplest form of camouflage is 'colour-matching'. Many caterpillars are green because they live and feed among green leaves, while creatures such as wolf spiders, scuttling about on the barc ground, are brown.

The shadow on the underside of an animal's body may give its position away, and so many animals also employ 'countershading'. The body is dark above but paler below and when seen from the side its solid, three-dimensional appearance is transformed, so that it looks like a flat object, difficult to spot initially or locate accurately. Deer and antelope have pale bellies for just this reason.

Many fish and sea birds go one better. Seen from below, the silvery underside of a fish becomes invisible against the brightness of the sea's surface. Viewed from above, the darker colours of the fish's back merge with the gloom of the ocean's depths. Similarly the pale belly plumage of a sea bird blends in

In the struggle for survival that continues in the wild, predators and prey have devised many ways of outwitting one another. It is a biological arms race and at any time either protagonist can be ahead. One successful strategy is to become 'invisible' simply by blending in with the background, a method that is practised by both hunter and hunted.

The tiger's stripes, for instance, look gaudy when seen in a zoo, but in its natural home in an Asian forest the colour

LIZARD COLOUR *Chameleons change colour according to the light and temperature.*

with the glare from the sky and the darker plumage on its back merges with the darker colour of the sea or rocks below.

Some animals go to amazing lengths to be inconspicuous; they very precisely imitate inanimate or inedible objects. Frogmouths are nocturnal birds, living in the forests of Australia and South-east Asia, that pass the day posing as branches – to the extent that their markings mimic the texture of peeling bark. Looper caterpillars, stick insects and some praying mantises look like twigs, while other mantises, katydids (a kind of tropical grasshopper), bush crickets and leaf insects resemble leaves – they even sport lifelike patterns of veins.

And when the real leaves have dropped from the tree and come to rest on the forest floor, there are horned frogs and a multitude of ground-dwelling insects that have adopted a mottled brown coloration to merge with the decomposing leaf litter in which they hide.

BLENDING IN *Flatfish change colour to fit in with their background.*

On the bottom of the sea, fish play the same cryptic game. The aptly named stonefish, for example – also notable for its venomous spines – looks remarkably like a stone, and the leafy sea dragon, a relative of the sea horse, resembles a piece of floating seaweed. Flatfishes, such as turbot and brill, are able to change the colour of their skin in order to match the colour and texture of the seabed on which they rest.

But what if the background changes?

An Arctic fox, willow grouse or snowshoe hare with pure white fur or feathers would be very conspicuous when the snow melts, so they solve the problem by changing colour – not instantly like the flatfish, but gradually modifying their coat or plumage in order to adapt to the changing seasons.

FOREST PROWLER *The tiger's stripes act as camouflage in tropical forests.*

In the spring, when the browns and greens of vegetation begin to appear but patches of snow still lie on the ground, these creatures moult most, but not all, of their white fur or feathers. By early summer, when the snow has disappeared completely, the animals have followed suit and are dressed in brown. When the snows of winter return they moult their summer coats and revert to pure white once more.

EXCEPTIONS TO THE RULE

Most snakes creep, but some can fly. Most birds fly, but some

can only walk or run – while a few can walk underwater.

There are even fish that thrive out of water and climb trees.

Nature has many surprises that break all the normal rules.

Humankind started using the wheel some 5000 years ago, but nature had discovered its properties long before we did, as well as those of cog or propeller-like mechanisms based on the wheel. In the minute world of microscopic organisms, for example, there are bacteria, such as *Escherichia coli* and *Salmonella*, that propel themselves along through water using hair-like 'paddles' known as flagella.

Escherichia coli has six flagella distributed around the outside of its sausage-shaped body. Each hair is attached to a tiny body in the bacterium's cell wall that resembles what can only be described as a 'rotary engine'. It is thrashed not from side to side but, surprisingly, in a circular motion like a propeller. When the movement is in an anticlockwise direction, the action drives the bacterium along at a speed equivalent to about 30 mph (48 km/h). For the hairs to rotate they must be attached to some sort of rotary joint or drive shaft.

Another surprise is that the motor driving the bacterium is powered by proton 'batteries'. The fuel comes from the nuclei of hydrogen atoms, moved around by electrical fields,

MIRACLE-WALKER *The basilisk (below) can skip its way across water. Previous pages: a horned frog blends in among the leaves of a Malaysian rain forest.*

and causing movement. A third surprise is that the creature does not whizz about at random. Instead, it runs along in a gently sweeping curve for about a second, stops and 'twiddles about' for a tenth of a second, then runs again in another direction. The 'twiddle' is achieved when the hairs rotate in a clockwise direction.

What many believed was no more than a primitive organism is, in fact, a remarkably complicated enigma.

RUNNING FAST TO WALK ON WATER

IF THE BASILISK LIZARD SLOWS DOWN IT SINKS BENEATH THE WATER

According to popular medieval legend, the basilisk was a dragon-like creature endowed with the terrible power to kill with a glance. The common basilisk, *Basiliscus basiliscus*, has no such ability, and only the crest worn on the head and back of the male links it to the legendary reptile.

Yet this lizard of tropical America,

which lives on plants and insects, does possess an amazing power: it can walk on water as well as on land. Standing on its hind legs – some species are up to 1 ft (30 cm) long – and moving with short leaps, it thrashes about on long scaly toes so fast that they give it a purchase on the water. With its body half upright and its tail angled backwards and upwards, it has been seen crossing 1300 ft (400 m) of open water at 7½ mph (12 km/h). The technique depends on momentum: if the basilisk slows down, it sinks and has to swim.

THE FLIGHTLESS BIRD THAT CAN SWIM, RUN AND JUMP

AUSTRALIA'S CASSOWARY CANNOT FLY, BUT HAS MANY SKILLS TO COMPENSATE

A bird that is as big as a smallish adult human being, that cannot fly but can outrun a dog, and that can kill a person with a blow from its claws, is clearly an exception to the general rule.

The Australian or southern cassowary (*Casuarius casuarius*) is one such creature. It is the largest of three species of cassowary and lives in the lowland rain forests of New Guinea, the nearby Indonesian islands of Ceram and Aru, and parts of Queensland in north-eastern Australia. At 110-143 lb (50-65 kg), it is a heavyweight, with wings

FATHER'S IN CHARGE *The male cassowary looks after the chicks.*

that are little more than stumps, and a few horny rods instead of quills. There is no tail, and the feathers are like stiff hairs.

Of the 9200-odd species of living birds, a tiny minority of about 45 cannot fly. These include aquatic penguins (family Spheniscidae), as well as the ostriches of south-west Africa and Asia (Struthionidae), the rheas of South America (Rheidae), kiwis of New Zealand (Apterygidae) and the emu (*Dromaius novaehollandiae*) and cassowary of Australia. Apart from the penguin, all these birds belong to a group known as 'ratites' which have lost the keeled sternum – or breastbone – that anchors the wing-muscles in ordinary birds. The penguin still needs strong wing muscles – but uses them to propel itself through water.

Although the cassowary cannot take to the sky, it is a strong swimmer and a powerful jumper and runner, able to reach speeds of around 30 mph (50 km/h). Its sturdy legs have three long toes – the inner one is up to 4 in (10 cm) long – and large claws. The claws are deadly, capable of inflicting fatal wounds on humans, although the cassowary is essentially a shy bird, preferring to go unnoticed.

The cassowary is instantly recognisable

two pairs of broad wings are each under separate control and can work independently. Their wing pitch is variable, and because of their size they can beat at a very low rate that allows for delicate adjustments – 20 beats per second, compared with the 200 beats of a housefly.

Dragonflies are also fast flyers. One Australian species was clocked at an astonishing 60 mph (96 km/h), albeit over a short distance.

FLIGHT WITHOUT FEATHERS OR WINGS

WEBBED CREATURES THAT
HAVE ADAPTED BY GLIDING

It is hard to imagine frogs, lizards and squirrels gliding through the air 40 ft (12 m) above the ground. But if a degree of flight will assist survival, then evolution

by the brightly coloured skin on its featherless head and the tall bony crest on its skull. It is also unusual for its parental habits: the male, which is smaller than the female, spends a month incubating the three to five green eggs, each just over 5 in (13 cm) long, and stays with the chicks for the first four months of their lives.

MASTERS OF AERIAL MANOEUVRABILITY

DRAGONFLIES WERE AMONG THE FIRST
INSECTS TO EVOLVE INTO FLIGHT

No other flying creature, or man-made aircraft, can equal the manoeuvrability of the dragonfly, among the earliest of insects to evolve flight – giant specimens fossilised in coal, with wingspans of 24 in (60 cm), date from about 300 million years ago. It can hover directly over a fixed point whichever way the wind is blowing, move in any direction, including backwards, and gain or lose height at will.

To perform these feats, dragonflies use a number of sophisticated techniques for controlling speed and orientation in response to prevailing conditions. First, their huge compound eyes, with as many as 30 000 facets, occupy most of their heads. In some cases, the eyes meet in the middle, giving the dragonfly all-round vision and thus enabling it to lock on to the slightest

movement and the smallest targets in its flying space. All the while, it is also recalculating its position, before zooming in on its flying prey, which it proceeds to scoop up with its three pairs of legs and then dissects with its jaws.

Secondly, specialised organs in the antennae measure the direction and speed of the wind. Finally, the dragonfly's

GLIDING TO SURVIVE
Among creatures that have learned how to glide are various species of possum (right) and lizard (below).

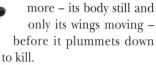

WINDHOVER
*The common kestrel
is one of nature's most
skilled hoverers.*

will often exploit the smallest advantages and a species will develop the beginnings of an ability to fly.

Several species of frogs have long fingers joined by webs broad enough to enable them to glide. The animal launches itself from high in a tree with its legs outstretched and its webs fully spread to break the fall. Crude though it seems, this system enables the little Borneo flying frog, *Rhacophorus pardalis*, $2^2/5$ in (6 cm) long, to leap almost 10 ft (3 m), or 50 times its own length. Another frog, *Hyla miliaris*, can glide at an incline of 18 degrees to the horizontal.

Various lizard species of the genus *Draco* in the tropical rain forests of Southeast Asia have also taken to gliding. The last five to seven ribs of these animals bear 'patagiums' – folds of skin that unfurl to form a heart-shaped fan when the ribs are spread outwards. The lizard now has a pair of stubby 'wings' to glide with, and uses its tail to increase and control the lift. Taking off from a height of 33 ft (10 m), one of the champions – the 'flying dragon' *Draco maximus* – can cover distances of 200 ft (60 m). It selects a landing site with great precision, and glides down to make a soft, safe landing.

All sorts of small mammals employ similar techniques. Among the marsupials, the sugar glider possum, *Petaurus breviceps*, of eastern Australia and New Guinea measures about 16 in (40 cm) from its nose to the tip of its long fluffy tail, which it uses as a rudder. It glides for distances of 165 ft (50 m) on the furry membrane stretched tightly between its outspread limbs. Bats, on the other hand, are genuine flyers that were already fully developed 50 million years ago. Other gliding mam-

mals include species of 'flying' squirrels in Europe and Asia (genus *Pteromys*) and in North America (genus *Glaucomys*).

HIGH-LEVEL VIEW FOR A GROUND-LEVEL FEAST

*KESTRELS HOVER IN THE AIR TO
FIND PREY AND SWOOP TO KILL*

Trees and telegraph poles are favourite perching places for the common kestrel, *Falco tinnunculus*, of Africa, Asia and Europe. But its special talent is to perch in the sky itself in order to scan the ground below. Because it feeds mostly on the ground – small mammals, insects, reptiles – it needs a high viewpoint.

When the wind is strong enough, the kestrel hangs motionless, facing the wind with its body horizontal and wings outstretched. When the air is still, it uses rapid downbeats of its wings to maintain altitude. The bird steers and balances by delicate shifts of its outspread tail feathers, and can hover over the same spot for a minute or

DIPPING DIVER *A dipper
plunges in for a watery meal.*

more – its body still and only its wings moving – before it plummets down to kill.

The falcon is one of the few daytime birds of prey in Europe that includes hovering as part of its standard repertoire. Other, less common birds that practise the same technique (such as little terns and some species of kingfisher) also have pointed wings and a fairly low weight – from about 2 to 7 oz (60 to 200 g). Hovering is just one part of the kestrel's arsenal of hunting ploys. It has super-effective eyesight, too. Its daytime vision is so acute that it can spot a beetle in the grass from a good 100 ft (30 m) up in the air, and then swoop down at 30 mph (48 km/h) to pounce on its victim.

FEATHERED AMPHIBIAN

*THE UNIQUE DIPPER CAN DIVE,
SWIM AND WALK UNDERWATER*

There are five species of dippers (*Cinclus cinclus*) that can be found in Europe, Asia, North Africa and North America, where it is sometimes called a water ouzel (*Cinclus mexicanus*). The dipper is a remarkable bird in that it is able to dive, swim – and walk along the bottom of a river.

Smaller than a blackbird, with a drab, sooty plumage and white on its throat and breast, the dipper is usually seen near the rushing streams it favors. Oblivious to the hazardous current, it alights on the surface of the river, is caught and bobs about like

SNAKES THAT PARACHUTE TO SAFETY

The golden tree snake of southern Asia, *Chrysopelea ornata*, is an expert climber, undeterred by tall or smooth-barked trees as it slides through the rain forest hunting for creatures such as frogs, lizards and small birds and mammals.

It also has long, tough muscles that enable it to 'fly'. It launches itself into the air at an angle of 30°, broadening and flattening its body and bracing its skeleton. During its fall, it hollows its stomach surface into a concave shape that captures air to create a 'drag', just as a parachute does. It shares this talent for flying with other golden tree snakes, such as *Chrysopelea paradisi* from Borneo – the most adept at flattening its body.

AIRBORNE *Flattening its body lets the golden tree snake 'fly'.*

cork, then dives head first into the clear water of a calm patch.

Using its small wings as flippers to swim to the bottom, it 'walks' on wide feet for several seconds along the bed of the stream, as easily as if it were in the open air, its body bent forward into the current. It feeds on caddis flies, snails and other crustaceans, worms, the odd water plant or two and the occasional small fish. When it is ready, it lets itself rise to the surface and drifts for a while with its wings slightly spread out to dry. It swallows the small prey in its beak, and then flies off.

Other birds seek out their food in rough waters. In the fast-flowing, white-water rapids of Andean rivers, the torrent duck dives into the most turbulent stretches in search of aquatic 'bugs' that thrive in the oxygen-rich waters. Similarly, the strikingly plumaged harlequin duck of North America and the blue duck of New Zealand not only rely on swift-flowing water to find food, but also allow the strong currents in gorges and the like to carry them out of reach of predators such as mink, rats and goshawk.

HOW TO BAFFLE A SHARK
To travel fast, or avoid pursuers, flying fish can jump right out of their oceanic world and glide for up to 10 seconds.

FISH THAT TAKE TO THE AIR

FLYING FISH LEAP FROM THE SEA TO GLIDE OVER THE WAVES

Flying fish have been known to leap 30 ft (10 m) and more on to the deck of a sea-going vessel. The flying fishes of the family Exocoetidae are not flyers who can stay airborne under their own power. But they are remarkably efficient gliders who can launch themselves into the air, and then take advantage of ocean updraughts to carry them along. 'Two-winged' species such as the common tropical flying fish, *Exocoetus volitans*, use their single pair of highly enlarged pectoral fins to glide. 'Four-winged' species such as the Californian flying fish, *Cypselurus californicus*, the largest in the family, about 18 in (45 cm) long, also have enlarged pelvic fins.

In order to propel themselves out of the water, flying fish pump their swimming speed up to nearly 30 mph (45 km/h) by vigorously beating their tails. The streamlined head and body start to emerge, while the long, broad pectoral fins stay retracted; the fish spreads them only when the lower fin is clear of the water. With a favourable wind, it can rise 10 ft (3 m) above the level of the sea and glide over 650 ft (200 m) for anything from 4 to 10 seconds. This take-off enables it to escape pursuing hunters by vanishing from their undersea world, but once in flight it cannot steer.

A few other fish, such as the flying gurnard, *Dactylopterus volitans*, which is

MUDSKIPPER *Bulges behind a lugubrious-looking face show where this amphibious fish carries its breathing gear.*

found in the warmer parts of the Atlantic, are also able to leap out of the water and glide – but for much shorter distances than flying fish. Of all the other 'flying' species, only the fresh-water hatchet fish or characin of South American waters, *Gastero-pelecus sternicla* (no relation of the deep-sea hatchet fish, but related to the piranha), can actually prolong its flight with rapid beats of its pectoral fins, buzzing a few inches above the water like an outsize insect.

Other flyers use their tail, like the flying fish, to scull across the water. The four-eyed fish from Central America, which has eyes that can see both above and below the water at the same time, escapes from danger from underwater predators by skimming over the water surface.

AT HOME BOTH IN AND OUT OF THE WATER

MUDSKIPPERS AND LUNGFISH BREATHE THROUGH GILLS OR LUNGS

Mudskippers, found on the tropical coasts of the Indian and Pacific oceans, are fish that can walk. They use elongated pelvic fins to walk on shore for hours at a time. They can even climb trees, skip around (hence their name) and, if needs be, 'run' faster than a human being.

The biggest mudskippers grow up to a foot (30 cm) long. They live in tidal man-grove swamps or mud flats, where they feed on insects, spiders, worms and small crustaceans and fish. Out of the water, they are able to breathe through their gills, since water is stored in their bulky heads – a kind of aqualung in reverse. The mud-skippers' adaptation to their terrestrial lifestyle is so advanced that they see better on land than they do in the water, are able

to gauge distance and contours, and can distinguish colours.

Whales and dolphins are mammals whose ancestors once left the water to live on land, but later found that they could do better back in the water. Other mammals, such as seals and otters, are aquatic predators, and even some birds – such as the penguin – have lost the power of flight, and taken to the ocean life again. But it is rarer to find fishes – whose distant ances-tors specialised for a life at sea – that have found the land a livable habitat.

In parts of Africa, South America and Australia, lungfish are able to survive periodic droughts since they have both gills and lungs. The Australian *Neoceratodus forsteri*, the barramundi of Queensland, with its large, lobe-like fins, survives in foul and stagnant waters where any other fish would suffocate, by coming to the surface to breathe through its single lung.

South American lungfish, or loalach, and the various *Protopterus* species of Africa have a pair of lungs and gills so elementary that if trapped underwater they would drown. They are eel-like fishes, whose fins have evolved into slender sensitive feelers. The largest of the African

species, *Protopterus aethiopicus*, found in East Africa, is a mottled yellow colour and grows up to 6½ ft (2 m) long.

In times of drought, the South American ones can burrow into mud and let it dry until they are wrapped in a hard clay ball. They may stay dormant like this for two or

DESERT SPIDERS TAKE TO THEIR WHEELS

On the sand dunes of the Namib Desert in south-western Africa lives the 'dancing white lady'. It is the spider *Carparchne aureoflava*, but it is no ordinary spider. When a predator, such as a hungry sand-diving lizard, threatens it and the spider is unable to run away easily over the cascading sand, it uses an ingenious routine to escape the danger. It simply folds its legs beneath its body and cartwheels down the steeply sloping slip-face of a dune at a speed of up to 30 mph (50 km/h). It is one of the few examples of wheel-like motion in nature.

three years, waiting for the rains to revive them. The African ones have mucous-lined cocoons that bake hard during a drought and allow them to survive in a similar way.

Lungfishes are living fossils that give clues to the sequence of events in which fish made the transition to land, more than 350 million years ago. Their presence

in three different continents is a relic of the days until about 135 million years ago when Australia, Africa and South America were part of the great southern continent called Gondwanaland.

THE ONLY BIRDS ABLE TO FLY IN REVERSE

HIGHLY DEVELOPED MUSCLES LET HUMMINGBIRDS HOVER WHEN FEEDING

Hummingbirds are the only birds able to fly in any direction – forwards, backwards, sideways – and to hover in a stationary position. The structure of their wings is different from that of other birds, longer in proportion to their body size, with a blade-like shape and a shoulder joint that allows the wing to be rotated in every plane. Hummingbirds also have the most highly developed musculature of all the vertebrates. According to the species, the wings beat at anything from 22 to 78 times per second, and may reach 200 beats per second in some males during courtship ceremonies. At this speed, their wings are an almost invisible blur, producing the characteristic humming noise that gives the family its English name.

This form of flying is extremely energy-intensive, and hummingbirds lose a lot of heat. Even in the warmth of the tropical

THE LIFE OF A NECTAR-SIPPER
Only tropical warmth and a diet of nectar allow the hummingbird to enjoy its high-energy style of living.

day, they have to feed nearly all the time to keep up their energy and body temperature. During the cool of the night, they fall into a deep torpor when their metabolism slows down and their body temperature falls until it is only just warmer than the surrounding air. Without this energy-saving device, they would lose more calories than they could replace.

The hummingbirds' vibrant flight is stationary when they hover in front of a

coarse hair, and has nostrils on the tip of its beak. The three species of kiwi are cousins of the moas – another New Zealand oddity that only became extinct during the last few centuries. They belong to a family of flightless birds that includes the ostrich, rhea, cassowary and emu.

Larger than chickens, with stubby wings that are too small to project above their plumage, the different kinds of kiwi feed at night on insects, berries and seeds, as well as on worms, grubs and slugs. These they catch by probing the ground with their flexible 6 in (15 cm) beaks.

Kiwis' small eyes do not cope well with daylight, but they have acute hearing and a particularly keen sense of smell. Their most distinctive feature, however, is the size of their eggs, which they lay underground in burrows. The female brown kiwi (*Apteryx australis*) weighs about 5³/4 lb (2.6 kg), for example, and produces eggs weighing nearly 1 lb (450 g) each – so large, in fact, that she has trouble walking before she lays them, one at a time at intervals of just over a month. The male does most of the incubating for about 10 to 12 weeks, during which time he leaves the nest for only a few minutes at a time to look for food if the female fails to provide it.

Stranded on the ground, kiwis are vulnerable to alien predators such as the cats and weasels brought in by European settlers. Numbers of the little spotted kiwi, in particular, have dwindled to about 1000, but there are now special laws in New Zealand to protect and conserve all kiwis.

WALKING ON WATER

The ability of the water bug *Gerris lacustris* to propel itself in quick bursts across the surface of ponds, lakes and quiet waters has earned it the common names of 'pond skater' and 'water strider'.

Water has a surface tension that is like an elastic film, strong enough to support the pond skater if it spreads its weight over a wide area. It extends its long middle and hind pairs of legs, sculling with the middle legs while steering with the hind pair. The front pair, shorter and thicker than the rest, are used to grasp prey – mainly small insects.

The underside of the insect's body and legs are tipped with pads of fine, waxy hairs with which it detects the presence of the insects. Their struggles as they fall on to the water cause vibrations in the surface film that are picked up by the hairs.

DECEPTIVE FRAGILITY *The pond skater darts after prey.*

EGG-LAYING CHAMPIONS
New Zealand's kiwi birds lay unusually large eggs, in relation to the mother's size.

flower to sip its nectar, their wings beating from back to front in an almost horizontal plane. In normal flight, both the upbeat and the downbeat phases provide propulsion and support, in contrast with other birds, where only the downbeat provides the power stroke.

GROUND-HOGGING KIWIS

OUTSIZE EGGS AND NOCTURNAL HABITS
DISTINGUISH NEW ZEALAND'S ODDITY

New Zealand's national bird, the kiwi, is one of nature's eccentrics – a nocturnal bird that cannot fly, has no tail, lays enormous eggs, has plumage that looks like

ATHLETES OF THE LAND, SEA AND AIR

The fastest, heaviest, nimblest, bounciest . . . the champions in nature's Olympics have strictly practical reasons for their prowess. Only by beating all others in their different fields have they managed to win the fight for survival.

The struggle for survival created nature's athletes. The fastest runners, highest jumpers and deepest divers in the animal world have achieved these distinctions as part of the great evolutionary race between hunter and hunted.

Predators track their targets and prey detect danger with sophisticated sensory systems. But when the watching and waiting are over and the time comes to move, they have to move fast. At the moment of capture, the pursuer in particular must be quicker than the pursued, although it might not use its entire body to achieve this superiority. Instead, it might use specialised limbs such as the agile forelimbs of the preying mantis or the lightning-fast, telescopic tongue of the chameleon.

One of the fastest known movements in the natural world is when a sea anemone or its relative a jellyfish discharges its stings. Each sting cell on a jellyfish's tentacles contains a coiled, barbed thread which shoots out at a speed of more

than 6½ ft per second (2 m/second) with an acceleration 40 000 times the force of gravity, and about 10 000 times that experienced by astronauts at take-off.

FLEET-FOOTED ELEGANCE

THE CHEETAH — THE SWIFTEST SPRINTER IN THE ANIMAL WORLD

The land-speed record for animals belongs to the sleek and agile cheetah with a top speed of 70 mph (110 km/h) – although like all sprinters it is a short-distance runner and cannot maintain the pace for more than 550 yd (500 m). Unlike the other cats, it hunts by pursuing prey in open grassland, rather than by stalking or ambushing. It is a technique that depends on its tremendous acceleration – 0 to 45 mph (72 km/h) in 2 seconds.

The cheetah goes for smaller, often very fleet-footed, prey such as gazelles,

THREE-TON FURY *A huge bulk, fearsome horn and notoriously bad temper make the black rhinoceros one of Africa's most formidable foes.*

impala antelopes and the calves of wildebeest. Having located a target group, it walks quietly forwards through the tall grass, gauging reactions, ready to pounce. Then it breaks into a canter, searching for the young, ageing or disabled animal that is easier to bring down.

When the victim starts to run, the pursuer goes into overdrive. It reaches 60 mph (100 km/h) in a few bounds, and in 200 to 300 yd (185 to 275 m) catches and bowls over the animal with a violent swipe of its paw followed by a choking grip on its throat. This frantic race lasts for only a few seconds, but the exhausted cheetah needs several minutes to regain its breath before it can feed. The secret of its speed derives from its long legs, flexible spine, powerful muscles, low weight – only 90 to 110 lb (40 to 50 kg) – and its non-retractable claws, which are unique among the cat family and give it greater traction.

It is not well equipped for self-defence, however, and can easily be driven from its kill by larger carnivores, such as lions, and by pack animals, such as the African hunting dog. In times of plenty, this is less likely to happen. But when drought and loss of habitat are putting all animals under pressure, as it is today throughout the cheetah's range from Africa to southwest Asia, there is trouble ahead for this solitary predator more expert at killing its prey than at defending its ownership.

THE HORNED JUGGERNAUT OF THE SAVANNAH

A SOLITARY BROWSER, THE BLACK RHINO IS UNPREDICTABLY DANGEROUS

Three tons of muscle, short but powerful legs, a rock-hard skull and a constant bad temper make the black rhinoceros, *Diceros bicornis*, a living bulldozer best left strictly alone. However, the tragedy of the rhino is the superstition that its horns have aphrodisiac qualities. For this, it has been mercilessly hunted by the only animal able

RECORD SPRINTER
Cheetahs can run three times faster than the fastest human.

to confront it safely – man behind the barrel of a gun.

In nature, every other creature respects and fears the black rhino. Its responses are notoriously unpredictable, and it does not hesitate to charge any intruder, including Jeeps and trains, with an agility surprising in so massive an animal. Immense strength and a top speed of up to 28 mph (45 km/h) make its charge one of unstoppable momentum. The shock of the impact alone would be lethal, and the attack is delivered with spasmodic head movements aimed at impaling or tossing the opponent with its two formidable horns, the front one up to 50 in (130 cm) long.

Only five species of rhino survive, all of them overhunted, in shrinking territories. In Africa the black rhino and white rhino (*Ceratotherium bicornis*) have smooth skins and two horns. Both the rare Javan rhino (*Rhinoceros sondaicus*) and the great Indian rhino (*Rhinoceros unicornis*) have a single horn and bumpy skin folded so that it looks patched together. The Sumatran rhino (*Didermocerus sumatrensis*), the only living species with a woolly coat, and

HANGING AROUND IN THE TREE TOPS

The sloth was well named after one of the 'seven deadly sins'. It is so lethargic that it eats, sleeps, mates and even gives birth while clinging upside down to a branch of a tree. Both three-toed and two-toed sloths live in the tropical rain forests of Central and South America, feeding largely on leaves. All have blunt muzzles, long, coarse fur that grows from belly to back and from toes to hips and shoulders, and long, powerful arms that end in massive curved claws.

During the eight or nine hours of the day when they are not resting, these mammals move very slowly, hanging by all four legs with their backs to the ground and their claws hooked over branches. They travel no faster than 650 to 980 ft (200 to 300 m) per hour, and one observer even witnessed a sloth making a journey of 125 ft (38 m) in 24 hours. They seldom venture on to the ground, but when they do, they have to drag themselves along on their bellies. When they swim, however, they can accelerate to roughly $1/3$ mile (500 m) per hour.

Sloths are a whole ecology in themselves, extraordinarily well adapted, despite their lethargic approach to life, to the rigours of their environment. Algae growing in tiny grooves and notches in their fur give them a tinge of green camouflage among the canopy of leaves. Ticks, fleas and other insects also live in the stable, furry habitat the sloth provides, including some moths that feed on the algae and whose life cycle is built around the sloth. Once a week, sloths venture to the ground to defecate. When they do, the female moth lays her eggs in the dung; the larvae feed and pupate there, hatch and then go looking for a mobile home of their own.

The distribution of sloths coincides fairly closely with that of their most dangerous predator, the harpy eagle (*Harpia harpyja*), which swoops through the trees of the forest canopy to tear its prey from the branches. It is even possible that the harpy eagle has strengthened its brawny legs and powerful talons and feet specifically to withstand the shock of ripping sloths loose from their branch holds.

SLOTHFUL HABITS *The sharp angles of a sloth's claws allow it to dangle freely from trees. On the whole, sloths avoid the ground, where they are too slow to be safe. They are more at ease in the water.*

the only Asian species with two horns, is also in decline.

Yet rhinos were among the most successful of all herbivore families during the Tertiary period that came between the fall of the dinosaurs and the modern age. The spectacular hornless *Indricotherium*, which lived 37 to 24 million years ago, was the biggest land mammal of all time, up to 18 ft (5.5 m) tall at the shoulder, and weighing 20 to 30 tons.

Mountain Athletes

THE CHAMOIS CAN NEGOTIATE ROCKY SLOPES WITH SURE-FOOTED EASE

One of the most graceful of all nature's athletes is the chamois – a cousin of the goat that has colonised several European mountain ranges from the Pyrenees to the Carpathians, and farther east into Asia Minor. In winter it favours alpine pastures and lower-lying areas. But in summer it ranges upwards to the snow-line, where it can climb and jump with nonchalant ease, indifferent to sheer drops along paths that are often impassable or downright invisible to humans.

Chamois have sharp eyes and a keen sense of smell. They are timid animals,

ALPINE ATHLETE *A chamois, cousin to the goat, leaps surefootedly from rock to rock in its high mountain habitat.*

easily startled into flight, when they can jump 13 to 16 ft (4 to 5 m) into the air, bouncing from rock to rock and using the narrowest overhangs as footholds. Yet even at headlong speed, they are so perfectly equipped for their dangerous habitat that they seldom lose their footing and fall. Their lack of a collarbone allows them to make very long strides, and their sturdy, muscular legs give them a powerful spring to move their weight – from 65 to 130 lb (30 to 60 kg).

The chamois' resilient hooves are cloven into two long-pointed 'toes', with sharp edges giving them extra purchase on the rocks. The curious hooked horns of the chamois are unique, curving backwards and downwards so sharply that it would be possible to hang them from a branch by their own horns.

Australia's Long-Distance Jumpers

POWERFUL HIND LEGS KEEP THE KANGAROO HOPPING

Australia's 52 species of kangaroo have a wide range of habitats, from open plains to marshland, forests to mountain regions. There is even a tree-dwelling kangaroo, genus *Dendrolagus*. The biggest of all are the great red kangaroos, *Macropus rufus*,

RUN WITH THE WIND *Red kangaroos lollop across Australia's open plains. Males are 6 ft (1.8 m) or more tall.*

which live on the open plains of Australia and are nearly 8 ft (2.4 m) tall. They spend most of their time browsing on all fours, but in emergencies can break into frantic flight with a series of giant two-legged bounds.

At full speed the red kangaroo can reach 30 mph (50 km/h), with record leaps 10 ft (3 m) high and 39 ft (12 m) long. It stretches its powerful hind legs, lowers its head and extends its strong muscular tail as a counterweight. But kangaroos cannot go flat out for long; their normal speed when travelling is between 9 and 12 mph (15 and 20 km/h), with leaps of 6 to 10 ft (2 to 3 m). Large kangaroos travel in groups, led by the biggest male.

Close relatives of the kangaroos are the rock wallabies that live mainly in the northern parts of Australia. They are smaller than kangaroos – the largest is no longer than 36 in (90 cm) excluding tail. They live amongst rocky outcrops and have feet that are specially adapted to agile climbing rather than to hopping across the plains. While their kangaroo relatives have extended claws on their hind feet to enable them to gain purchase on the flat ground, rock wallabies get their thrust from friction generated between the rock and the rough, grainy skin and fringes of coarse hair on their feet.

Another relative, the nailtail wallaby, runs along on its hind legs with its forelegs moving in a circle, a habit that has earned it the name of 'organ-grinder'.

THE RAIN FOREST'S TRAPEZE ARTISTS

SPIDER MONKEYS WALK, SWING AND LEAP THROUGH THE TREETOPS

Spider monkeys are high-level trapeze artists, moving through the rain forest treetops with consummate ease. The four species of spider monkeys (genus *Ateles*) use every technique of locomotion, from four-legged walking on top of the branches to two-armed swinging beneath them.

In this, the monkeys of South America are assisted by a remarkable tail that is like a fifth limb, supporting and stabilising the monkey while it feeds, travels or dangles upside down. The undersurface of the tail's lower third is naked of fur and has sensitive nerve endings, enabling the

FALL-SAFE *A South American spider monkey keeps its tail coiled around a handy branch – in case of emergencies.*

monkey to grip a branch tightly or handle fruit with utmost delicacy. Spider monkeys owe their common name to their very long limbs and tails, up to 35 in (90 cm) long.

Sometimes a monkey will launch itself into space – arms and legs outstretched in a 33 ft (10 m) dive on to a slender branch in the next tree. The animal's very long fingers give it a firm grip, though in moments of panic it occasionally misses its hold and plummets to the ground with a crash of broken branches.

These gymnasts of the forest canopy are so confident in their own speed and elusiveness that they make little effort to conceal themselves. They will scream and bark at intruders, throw dead branches, and even defecate derisively from the heights above. The four species are the Central American or black-handed spider monkey (*Ateles geoffroyi*), white-bellied or long-haired spider monkey (*Ateles belzebuth*), brown-headed spider monkey (*Ateles fusciceps*), and black spider monkey (*Ateles paniscus*).

Spider monkeys are generally no more than 23 in (58 cm) long, but in 1920 the Swiss geologist François de Loys claimed to have shot a specimen in the forests along the Venezuela-Colombia border that measured an astonishing 5 ft (1.5m) in length. No one since that time has been able to confirm de Loys' finding, and some now believe it to have been a hoax.

MUSCULAR WEIGHLIFTERS OF THE INSECT WORLD

ANTS CAN CARRY LOADS 30 TIMES HEAVIER THAN THEY ARE

To the casual observer, ants look like fragile insects with narrow waists and spindly legs, weighing at most only a minute fraction of an ounce. Close observation, however, reveals a family of champion weightlifters able to shift loads 20 to 30

PULLING THEIR WEIGHT *Ants heave together to shift a dead lizard.*

times heavier than they are in their powerful jaws. Mass for mass, these insects are proportionally 30 to 40 times stronger than a horse.

Muscle power is usually defined as the amount an animal can lift for every square inch of muscle. Seen in this way, the difference between vertebrates and insects is not so great. For instance, a human being might be strong enough to exert a force of 85 to 142 lb for every square inch of muscle (6 to 10 kg for every square centimetre), while an ant's jaw muscles can manage from 57 to 100 lb per sq in (4 to 7 kg/cm^2). The difference is that insects have two or three times more muscles than a human, which means they have less to do to support a load, and more spare capacity for other tasks.

Ants are remarkable in other ways, too, with the most sophisticated social structures of any insect apart from bees. Like bees, most species of ants divide up into three groups or castes: the queen, whose job is to lay eggs; female workers, who look after the nest; and slightly larger male soldier ants who defend it. Some, such as

DEADLY LOOKOUT *Conspicuous on its thorn-bush prop, the black mamba is so deadly it need not fear being seen.*

the African *Bothriomyrmex decapitans*, have distinctly imperialist habits and survive by 'enslaving' other species. A queen *Bothriomyrmex decapitans* allows herself to be taken into a nest belonging to *Tapinoma* ants. She bites off the head of the *Tapinoma* queen, and then starts laying her own eggs, with *Tapinoma* slaves to look after them.

AFRICA'S DEADLY BLACK MAMBA

THE SNAKE WITH A LETHAL BITE AND AN ALARMING TURN OF SPEED

In the African bush and the savannahs south of the Sahara, few snakes are more feared than the black mamba, *Dendroaspis polylepis*, with a slender body up to 14 ft

(4.3 m) long, and a bite that injects a lethal venom attacking the nervous system. When angered, it becomes highly aggressive and may give chase at an alarming speed for a snake: some estimates go up to 12 mph (20 km/h) and more.

Young mambas often live in trees. As they grow heavier they move down to the ground, where they travel by sideways undulations like other members of their family, such as cobras and coral snakes. The black mamba is the undisputed champion in its category, however. Heavier, bulkier snakes such as vipers and rattlesnakes can manage little more than 2 mph (3 km/h), while the slimmer cobras reach 3$\frac{1}{2}$ to 5 mph (6 to 8 km/h).

When catching its prey, the cave racer

READY TO JUMP *The flea's hind legs have 'springs' of compressed protein, waiting to be triggered for a jump.*

snake from South-east Asia does not travel at all. Instead it coils its body around a convenient stalactite in a narrow cave passage and reaches out rapidly to grab bats and cave swiftlets as they fly past.

THE ELASTIC HIGH-JUMPER

THE FLEA CAN JUMP MORE THAN 100 TIMES ITS OWN LENGTH

When it takes off, a flea can achieve a speed of some 50 mph (80 km/h) – a rate of acceleration that would break a human being's leg. As in other insects, the jumping muscles are sited close to the joint between the flea's hind legs and thorax. When the flea draws up its legs before jumping, it activates a pair of ratchets that compress and contain the force of a rubbery protein called resilin, located in the pleural arc – the equivalent of our groin.

The action is like cocking a trigger or compressing a spring. The muscles near this joint are aligned with the pad of resilin, so that the slightest movement triggers the ratchet to release the stored energy of the resilin, instantly straightening the femur and catapulting the flea upwards at an extraordinary speed for so small an insect. Fleas average about $\frac{1}{8}$ in (3 mm) long, and can jump over 12 in (30 cm) – 100 times their own length. If a man could perform a similar feat, he would be able to jump more than three times the height of Nelson's Column in London's Trafalgar Square, from a standing start.

Similar in approach are the 7000-odd species of click beetle, measuring about

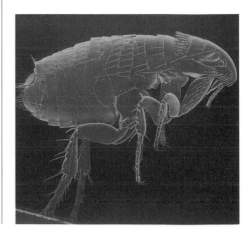

POWER IN RESERVE *A lurking trout can leap agilely out of the water to take a grab at any passing prey.*

½ in (1.3 cm) long. A click beetle does not use its legs to jump, but can jackknife its entire body to propel it up to 12 in (30 cm) into the air to escape predators.

SWIFT AND STREAMLINED

POWERFUL MUSCLES MAKE THE RIVER TROUT A SPEEDY PREDATOR

The brown trout, *Salmo trutta fario*, has a streamlined body and powerful tail muscles that enable it to swim against strong currents during migrations. In still water it can swim at nearly 20 mph (30 km/h) or, at the other extreme, stay motionless against the current. The predatory trout waits in ambush behind rocks or branches drooping in the water and leaps on to its prey in a few hundredths of a second. Sometimes it will even jump clear of the water to catch an insect flying near the surface.

SURFACE WATER GLIDER

THE FIERCE-LOOKING GIANT MANTA RAY IS A HARMLESS FILTER-FEEDER

Tales used to be told of giant manta rays (*Manta birostris*) that wrapped pearl fishers in their powerful black or brown folds and then devoured them. But despite a ferocious name and appearance, the giant manta ray or devilfish, found in the temperate and tropical Atlantic, eats nothing bigger than shrimps, filtering the tiny crustaceans and plankton through its specially adapted mouth.

With a wingspan of over 20 ft (6 m) and weighing up to 1½ tons, it is an aerobatic performer of tremendous power. After reaching a speed of 6 to 12 mph (10 to 20 km/h), it uses its winglike pectoral fins to leap more than 13 ft (4 m) above the surface, the tips of the fins flexed skywards. It travels as far as its launch speed will carry it, since its fins are neither big enough nor strong enough to give it a gliding capability. It then bellyflops into the water with a mighty smack and splash.

Manta rays are ovoviviparous: that is, the egg hatches inside the mother's body. The female giant manta ray has one large embryo; the largest on record was 50 in (1.3 m) wide and weighed 20 lb (9 kg).

The ray gets its name from *manta*, the Spanish word for 'cloak' – a reference to its cloak-like appearance. Its English name 'devilfish', it owes to the two horn-like fins on either side of its head. These form a funnel or tube when the fish is feeding, channelling food into the gaping mouth. Some other manta rays are less benevolent than the giant, with stinging spines in their long tails. The smallest ray is the stingless Australian *Mobula diabolis*, only 2 ft (60 cm) across.

DEEP-SEA DIVERS

SPERM WHALES CAN STAY SUBMERGED FOR WELL OVER AN HOUR

One day in 1932, the crew of the cable ship *All America* had to retrieve a telegraph cable from a depth of more than 3300 ft (1000 m). The load was unexpectedly heavy, and when it eventually surfaced, a fully grown sperm whale or cachalot, *Physeter macrocephalus*, was entangled in the cable.

Scientists now know that this huge marine mammal, which grows up to 70 ft (21 m) long and may weigh up to 60 tons, can dive much deeper than that. Sonar has detected sperm whales at depths of over 6560 ft (2000 m).

Sperm whales are the largest of the group of toothed whales that hunt large prey. They dive after octopus, cuttlefish and giant squid of the genus *Architeuthis*, which generally live at depths of more than 1650 ft (500 m) below sea level, and which they locate with their own version of sonar. Sperm whales can remain submerged for well over an hour.

A sperm whale's head occupies about a

SEA WINGS *Giant manta rays bask beneath the ocean waves.*

GIANT HUNTERS *Sperm whales dive thousands of feet beneath the sea's surface to prey on giant squid.*

third of its entire body, and contains a huge cavity that holds up to 5 tons of spermaceti, a liquid wax. According to one theory, this helps the whale to dive. As it goes deeper and the water temperature drops, the wax solidifies, becoming denser than the water and thus tending to sink. On the way up, according to this theory, the wax becomes liquid again and expands, making the whale more buoyant.

The sperm whale's respiratory system is much more efficient than a human being's, using about 10 per cent of the oxygen in the air in its lungs, compared with our 4 per cent. This is because its blood stores large amounts of oxygen, as do all its muscles, which are very rich in myoglobin, an oxygen-binding protein. As a result,

sperm whales can store twice as much oxygen dioxide in their muscles than land mammals can. They also have collapsible lungs that force air into the nasal passages and windpipes to prevent it from being absorbed by the body.

FAST AND FEARSOME

SWORDFISH, MARLIN AND SAILFISH –
THE WORLD'S FASTEST SWIMMERS

Some of the world's fastest swimmers belong to the group known as billfishes – sometimes weighing 880 lb (400 kg) or more, but scything through the waves at over 50 mph (80 km/h). They include the swordfish (*Xiphias gladius*), credited with a record speed of 60 mph (96 km/h), marlins (*Makaira*) and other sailfish (*Istiophorus*).

BILLFISH *A superbly athletic marlin leaps clear of the water.*

The swordfish's body is shaped like a rocket. Its toothless upper jaw is stretched into a flat sharp beak, measuring nearly a third of the fish's total length; its caudal fin

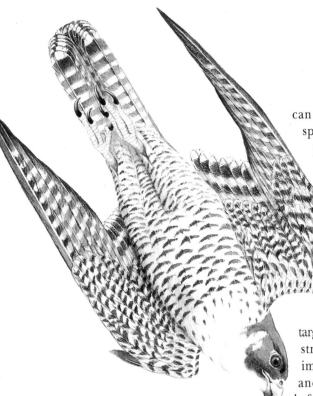

A PEREGRINE STOOPS *Its dive will end in a mid-air collision, a burst of feathers and death to its victim.*

is highly developed, and its streamlined tail powerfully muscled. With its retractable dorsal and pelvic fins, it looks like a blueprint for hydrodynamic perfection.

Swordfish inhabit the Atlantic and Pacific, as well as the Mediterranean and Black Sea. They have the strength and stamina to cover great distances following shoals of prey, which include sardines and mackerels, themselves able to travel at over 19 mph (30 km/h). Swordfish rise into the shoal from below and flail about with their 'sword' to stun or pierce their prey. They have even been known to damage small boats in their violence.

Marlins, too, are rovers, found in all the world's oceans, feeding near the surface on other fish. Like swordfish, they are much prized by game fishermen.

FEATHERED THUNDERBOLT

THE POWERFUL PEREGRINE STRIKES WITH LIGHTNING PRECISION

The peregrine falcon is the fastest bird in the world, reaching its greatest speed when diving or 'stooping' on a prey. Crows, pigeons or seabirds frantically try to flee, but once the falcon has 'locked' on to a bird, the end is almost inevitable. No prey can outfly the lightning speed of this powerful predator – believed to be up to 112 mph (180 km/h), depending on the angle at which it dives. As its quarry makes for cover, the peregrine launches itself into a steep power-dive, free-falling for hundreds of feet to intercept its target in a mid-air collision. It uses its strong hind claw like a lance, the impact breaking the victim's back and sending it plummeting, dead before it hits the ground. Peregrines rarely attack grounded or perching birds.

FLYING HIGH OVER AFRICA

HIGH AIR CURRENTS LIFT RUPPELL'S GRIFFON ABOVE ITS COMPETITORS

Rüppell's griffon, the commonest vulture in western Africa, soars above the savannah for long periods while foraging for food. It rides the air currents effortlessly until it spots the carcass of a dead mammal, usually already surrounded by jostling carrion-feeders, and then glides down to join the feast. Gliding like this, the griffon can cover tens of miles without flapping its wings – a feature that allows it the most accurate flying control and loses it very little altitude for the distance covered.

Usually, Rüppell's griffon has no need to soar very high to locate food – no more than about 13 000 ft (4000 m). However, in November 1973, one collided with an airliner near Abidjan, Ivory Coast, at an altitude of 36 988 ft (11 274 m), damaging one of the aircraft's engines.

Mammals cannot live permanently above about 30 000 ft (9000 m), but birds have no such handicap. Their respiratory system has a different structure. The body cavity is packed with a series of paired air sacs that are pumped like bellows by the action of flying, forcing air through a system of lung tubes that enable the oxygen to be used much more efficiently.

RIDING HIGH *Vultures can drift for miles on rising air.*

Radar observation has shown that small birds the size of a chaffinch will sometimes fly at heights of over 13 000 ft (4000 m) during migration, even when they have no mountains to cross.

AN UNLIKELY AQUABAT

A LUMBERING FLIGHT HIDES THE SKILLS OF AN EXPERT DIVER

The American brown pelican, *Pelecanus occidentalis*, looks ungainly, but has the accuracy of a guided missile when it plunges into the sea in search of prey. It is exceptional among the pelicans because it fishes by diving from the air rather than the surface. It usually dives from a height of 10 to 33 ft (3 to 10 m). It tilts, folds its wings, points its long beak and skilfully adjusts its direction as it hurtles in on its prey. Diving no more than $6^{1}/_{2}$ ft (2 m), it scoops fish into its large pouch, with its capacity of around $2^{1}/_{4}$ gallons (10 litres), and then swallows them after it has surfaced.

MISSILES *Brown pelicans hurtle downwards to skewer underwater targets.*

PICTURE CREDITS

3 OSF/Steve Turner. 6 Ardea London Ltd/E. Mickleburgh. 7 Heather Angel, T; Planet Earth Pictures/Robert Hessler, B. 8 Planet Earth Pictures/Peter David, T; Ardea London Ltd/Ferrero-Labat, B. 9 Planet Earth Pictures/ Sean T. Avery, T; Science Photo Library/Simon Fraser, B. 10 FLPA/T. Whittaker, T; Science Photo Library/David Parker, B. 11 Science Photo Library/Prof. Stewart Lowther, TL; Robert Harding Picture Library/Tony Waltham, TR; FLPA/David Hosking, B. 12 NHPA/Daniel Heuclin, T; FLPA/Eric and David Hosking, B. 12-13 Robert Harding Picture Library/Explorer. 13 Bruce Coleman Ltd/John Cancalosi, TL; Planet Earth Pictures/James D.Watt, TR. 14 NHPA/Norbert Wu. 15 Bruce Coleman Ltd/David Hughes, TL; Bruce Coleman Ltd/Keith Gunnar, TR; Bruce Coleman Ltd/Dr Sabine M. Schmidt, B. 16 Ardea London Ltd/Kenneth W. Fink, T; Heather Angel, B. 17 Life File/David Bayliss, T; Zefa Pictures, B. 19 Zefa Pictures/Boesch. 20 Zefa Pictures/Darodents. 22 Jacana/François Gohier. 23 Zefa Pictures/Erwin Christian. 24-25 Jacana/Jean-Paul Ferrero. 26 Magnum/Hiroji Kubota, L; Explorer/Jacques Brun, R. 27 Jacana/Jerry Schad, T; Jacana/D. Parer & E. Parer-Cook, B. 28-29 Bruce Coleman Ltd/Dieter and Mary Plage. 30 Robert Harding Picture Library/Gavin Hellier. 31 Robert Harding Picture Library/Gavin Hellier, L; OSF/Konrad Wothe, R. 32 Zefa Pictures. 33 Jacana/Frank S. Balthis. 34-35 Robert Harding Picture Library/Geoff Renner, T; 34-35 Robert Harding Picture Library/Nakamura, B. 35 Zefa Pictures. 36 Fred Bruemmer. 37 Life File/Fraser Ralston, T; GeoScience Features Picture Library/W. Higgs, B. 39 Zefa Pictures. 40-41 Zefa Pictures. 42 Robert Harding Picture Library/G.M. Wilkins. 43 Ardea London Ltd/D.Parer & E. Parer-Cook, L; Zefa Pictures, R. 44 Zefa Pictures. 45 NHPA/Rod Planck, L; Ardea London Ltd/D. Parer & E. Parer-Cook, R. 46 Planet Earth Pictures/J.R. Bracegirdle. 46-47 Bruce Coleman Inc./Giorgio Gualco. 48-49 Bruce Coleman Inc./Giorgio Gualco. 50-51 Jacana/Auscape. 51 Ardea London Ltd/François Gohier. 52 Ardea London Ltd/Adrian Warren. 52-53 Zefa Pictures. 54 Robert Harding

Picture Library/Robert Estall, T; Zefa Pictures/H. Armstrong, B. 55 Gerhard & Waltraud Klammet. 56 The Image Bank/Leo Mason, T; The Telegraph Colour Library, B; 57 Ardea London Ltd/François Gohier, T; Science Photo Library/Pekka Parviainen, B. 58 Ardea London Ltd/François Gohier. 59 Robert Harding Picture Library/G.R. Richardson, TL; Robert Harding Picture Library/Adina Tovy, CL; Bruce Coleman Ltd/Paul R. Wilkinson, BL; Ardea London Ltd/Jean-Paul Ferrero, TR; Zefa Pictures/Eugen, CR; NHPA/A.N.T./ Peter McDonald, BR. 60 Zefa Pictures, T; Science Photo Library/Alfred Pasicka, B. 61 Loren McIntyre. 62 Bruce Coleman Ltd/Gene Ahrens, T; Zefa Pictures/Damm, B. 62 63 Comstock/Dr. Georg Gerster. 64 Tom Stack and Associates/Kevin Schafer, T; Science Photo Library/Dick Rowan, B. 65 Bruce Coleman Ltd/Dr. Eckart Pott, TL; Tom Stack and Associates/Kevin Schafer, TR; Innerspace Visions/Doug Perrine, BL; U.S. Geological Survey/E.A. Shinn, BR. 67 Sunset/Weatherstock. 68-69 Science Photo Library/Pekka Parviainen. 69 Zefa Pictures. 70 Ciel et Espace/A. Fujii, T; Science Photo Library/Starlight/Roger Ressmeyer, B. 71 GeoScience Features Picture Library/F.Taylor. 72 Zefa Pictures. 73 Science Photo Library/Gordon Garradd. 74 Studio X/M. Engler/Bilderberg. 75 Science Photo Library/Royal Observatory, Edinburgh, T; Science Photo Library/Pekka Parviainen, B. 76 Zefa Pictures. 77 NHPA/G. J. Cambridge, T; Bruce Coleman Ltd/Andy Purcell, B. 78 Jacana/Pat Wild. 79 Bruce Coleman Ltd/Stephen J. Krasemann. 80 Bruce Coleman Ltd/Peter Ward, T; Heather Angel, BL; OSF/Patti Murray, BR. 81 Biofotos/Brian Rogers. 82 Jacana/Sylvain Cordier, TL; Bios/Bruno Pambour, TR; OSF/Scott Camazine, CL; OSF/Michael Fogden, CR; FLPA/Ian Rose, BL; OSF/Michael Fogden, BR. 83 OSF/Michael Fogden. 84 NHPA/David Woodfall. 85 OSF/Andy Park, TL; OSF/Harold Taylor, TR; Bruce Coleman Ltd/Michel Viard, B. 86 Tom Stack and Associates/Jeff Foott, L; Ardea London Ltd/Peter Steyn, TR; Bruce Coleman Inc./Kenneth W. Fink, BR. 87 Jacana/François Gohier, T; Planet Earth Pictures/William M. Smithey, Jr., B. 88 Claude Nuridsany and Marie Pérennou. 89 Bios/Klein-Hubert. 90 OSF/T.C. Middleton, L; OSF/Kjell Sandved, TR; Heather Angel, BR. 91

Bruce Coleman Ltd/Eric Crichton, T; Nature Photographers/Brinsley Burbidge, B. 92 Bruce Coleman Ltd/Luiz Claudio Marigo, T; Planet Earth Pictures/Margaret Welby, CL; NHPA/G.I. Bernard, CR; Bruce Coleman Ltd/Marie Read, B. 93 Heather Angel, T; Heather Angel, CL; FLPA/A. Wharton, CR; OSF/Deni Bown, B. 94 NHPA/A.P. Barnes, L; Bruce Coleman Ltd/Dr. Frieder Sauer, R. 95 Bruce Coleman Ltd/Hans Reinhard. 96 OSF/J.A.L. Cooke, T; Planet Earth Pictures/Nick Greaves, B. 97 Bios/Visage/Alain Compost. 98 OSF/Phil Devries, T. Bruce Coleman Ltd/Hans Reinhard, B. 99 Bruce Coleman Ltd/Michel Viard. 100 OSF/David and Sue Cayless, T; A-Z Botanical Collection/Elsa M. Megson, B. 101 OSF/Michael Fogden. 102-103 NHPA/A.N.T./Otto Rogge. 103 Planet Earth Pictures/Robert Canis. 104-105 Jacana/Jean-Paul Ferrero. 106 Heather Angel. 107 NHPA/A.N.T./P. German. 108 Bruce Coleman Ltd/Hans Reinhard. 108-109 Claude Nuridsany and Marie Pérennou. 110 Bruce Coleman Ltd/Kim Taylor, L; Bruce Coleman Ltd/Gerald Cubitt, R. 111 Bruce Coleman Ltd/Eric Crichton, T; Claude Nuridsany, B. 112 Bios/Roland Seitre, T; Jacana/Norbert Wu, C; OSF/Deni Bown, BL; Jacana/Norbert Wu, BR. 113 Bios/Michel Gunther, T; DRK Photo/Pat O'Hara, B. 114 NHPA/A.N.T. 115 OSF/Rudie H. Kuiter, L; OSF/Max Gibbs, R. 116 OSF/Babs and Bert Wells. 117 NHPA/Karl Switak, L; Bruce Coleman Inc./E.R. Degginger, R. 118 Bios/Alain Compost. 119 Bruce Coleman Ltd/John Markham, L; Bruce Coleman Inc./Cliff B. Frith, R. 120 Bruce Coleman Ltd/Michael Fogden. 120-121 DRK Photo/Larry Ulrich. 121 NHPA/Anthony Bannister, T; OSF/David G. Fox, B. 122 OSF/Frithjof Skibbe, T; NHPA/Stephen Dalton, B. 123 NHPA/Norbert Wu. 124 Nature Photographers/Paul Sterry. 125 Bruce Coleman Ltd/John Cancalosi, T; Bruce Coleman Inc./George B. Schaller, CL and CR; NHPA/Daniel Heuclin, B. 126 OSF/Animals Animals/B. Kent, T; NHPA/A.N.T./ Fenton Walsh, B. 127 NHPA/Anthony Bannister. 128 OSF/Animals Animals/Zig Leszczynski, T AND C; Thomas Eisner/Daniel Aneshansley, B. 129 OSF/Michael Fogden. 130 DRK Photo/Stephen J. Krasemann. 130-131 DRK Photo/Stephen J. Krasemann. 132 OSF/Animals Animals/Zig Leszczynski, T; DRK Photo/Stephen J.

Krasemann, C; Bruce Coleman Ltd/Geoff Dore, B. 133 Bios/Jean-Yves Grospas, T; OSF/Animals Animals/Zig Leszczynski, B. 134 Bruce Coleman Ltd/ Gerald Cubitt. 135 Bruce Coleman Ltd/Jane Burton, T; Bruce Coleman Ltd/Jean-Pierre Zwaenepoel, C; Bruce Coleman Ltd/Dr. Frieder Sauer, B. 136-137 Bruce Coleman Ltd/Michael Fogden.138-139 NHPA/Stephen Dalton. 139 Bruce Coleman Ltd/C.B. and D.W. Frith. 140 Bruce Coleman Ltd/Felix Labhardt, T; Bruce Coleman Inc./Cliff B. Frith, BL; NHPA/A.N.T., BR. 141 Bruce Coleman Ltd/Konrad Wothe. 142 Bruce Coleman Inc./C.B. and D.W. Frith, T; Bruce Coleman Inc./Jane Burton, B. 143 Bruce Coleman Ltd/Jane Burton. 144 145 DRK Photo/Michael Fogden. 145 OSF/Larry Crowhurst, C; Bruce Coleman Ltd/Frances Furlong, B. 146-147 OSF/Rafi Ben-Shahar. 147 Bruce Coleman Inc/Tom Brakefield. 148 Bios/Jany Sauvanet, L; Bruce Coleman Ltd/Michael Fogden, CR; OSF/Michael Fogden, BR. 149 Bruce Coleman Inc./Michael Fogden. 150 Bruce Coleman Inc./Jen and Des Bartlett, T; NHPA/Manfred Danegger, B. 151 DRK Photo/Wayne Lynch, T; Bruce Coleman Ltd/Konrad Wothe, B. 152 NHPA/Anthony Bannister, T; Science Photo Library/David Scharf, B. 153 Bruce Coleman Ltd/Michel Roggo, T; Bios/Yves Lefevre, B; 154 Jacana/Gerard Soury, T; Bruce Coleman Ltd/Frank Lane/Van Nostrand, B. 155 FLPA/Eric and David Hosking, T; FLPA/A.R. Hamblin, B.